Dieting

Other books in the Issues That Concern You series:

ISSUES THAT CONCERN YOU

Dieting

Claire Kreger Boaz, *Book Editor*

Christine Nasso, *Publisher*
Elizabeth Des Chenes, *Managing Editor*

GREENHAVEN PRESS

An imprint of Thomson Gale, a part of The Thomson Corporation

THOMSON

™

GALE

Detroit • New York • San Francisco • San Diego • New Haven, Conn. • Waterville, Maine • London • Munich

© 2008 Thomson Gale.

Star Logo is a trademark and Gale and Greenhaven Press are registered trademarks used herein under license.

For more information, contact
Greenhaven Press
27500 Drake Rd.
Farmington Hills, MI 48331-3535
Or you can visit our Internet site at http://www.gale.com

LIBRARY OF CONGRESS CATALOGING-IN-PUBLICATION DATA
Dieting / Claire Kreger Boaz, book editor.
p. cm. — (Issues that concern you)
Includes bibliographical references and index.
ISBN 978-0-7377-3644-1 (hardcover)
1. Reducing diets. 2. Weight loss. I. Boaz, Claire Kreger, 1973-
RM222.2.D562 2008
613.2'5—dc22
2007035368

Printed in the United States of America

CONTENTS

According to the American Obesity Association, 64.5 percent of Americans are obese and need to lose weight. Obesity related deaths claim more than three hundred thousand people annually, and America is quickly becoming the fattest nation on Earth. According to the Centers for Disease Control and Prevention (CDC), one of the national health objectives is to decrease the number of obese Americans by 15 percent by the year 2010, yet the number of overweight kids and adults continues to grow. One way health professionals are combating this escalating fat crisis is through widespread use of diet pills.

The use of diet pills is controversial, because there is little evidence to support their effectiveness. In fact, some diet pills are dangerous and pose a higher risk to the individual than being overweight.

On June 15, 2007, the first-ever diet pill approved by the Food and Drug Adminstration (FDA) became available over-the-counter without a prescription. The over-the-counter version, however, is one-half the strength of the prescription version. The manufacturer of the pill, called Allí (pronounced *ally*), claims that the drug works by blocking the body's absorption of one-fourth of all the fat consumed. The company is clear, however, that the pill will not work on its own, and it recommends a low-calorie diet and regular exercise to maximize weight loss. Still, advertisements claim that Allí will cause dieters to lose up to 50 percent more weight than dieters who do not use the drug.

According to the National Association to Advance Fat Acceptance (NAAFA), however, "ninety percent of all dieters regain some or all of the weight originally lost and at least one-third gain more." Americans are obsessed with finding a new way to diet with minimal effort, although studies show over and over that most people gain back all or more of the weight lost. Still, women are the main consumer base for the diet industry, and

Displays like this one may be a contributing factor to both adult and childhood obesity.

this continues to be true with Allí. According to the National Institute of Nutrition, 81 percent of female high school students want to lose weight, 49 percent of whom are underweight. Most of these young girls report they will "try anything" to lose weight, including weight-loss drugs.

ABC News reported on February 15, 2007, that the anticipated release of Allí had experts concerned because, "it isn't uncommon for those suffering from bulimia to abuse laxatives. Anorexics have also been known to take insulin-blocking drugs to suppress their hunger." Therapist David Drajkowski, told ABC News that, "I would think this could generate more people with diet disorders . . . or cause more disordered thinking."

According to a report that aired on CBS News on December 1, 2006, Americans spend more than $35 billion per year on diet products. The industry is able to thrive because most dieters will continue to try different diets and/or products because previous ones failed them. Teenage girls are particularly vulnerable to advertiser's claims about over-the-counter diet drugs.

The National Alliance on Mental Illness (NAMI) reports that "one reason younger women are particularly vulnerable to eating disorders is their tendency to go on strict diets to achieve an 'ideal' figure. This obsessive dieting behavior reflects today's societal pressure to be thin, which is seen in advertising and the

Many physicians are taking the steps necessary to become healthy role models for their patients.

media." A 2002 Federal Trade Commission (FTC) report showed that 55 percent of weight-loss products advertised failed to live up to their claims—yet people are continuously drawn to the promise of easy weight loss—even to the detriment of their health.

The list of health risks for diet pills is long. Drugs that are stimulant based are highly addictive and cause the user to want to increase the dosage once he or she becomes used to the way the drug works. The most frequently reported side effects of over-the-counter diet pills are nervousness, tremors, diarrhea, bulging eyes, racing heartbeat, and elevated blood pressure. In more extreme cases, long-term use of diet pills can even result in death.

Diet pills were popularized in the 1960s and 1970s. They were primarily in the amphetamine family and known as "speed." Speed's addictive properties quickly became a problem, and doctors quit prescribing diet drugs derived from amphetamines. In 1973 the FDA approved the drug fenfluramine, only to issue a recall on it and dexfenfluramine (fen-phen) in 1997 after reports of often irreversible damage to users' heart valves—sometimes the damage was severe enough to cause death.

Users of Allí report experiencing nasty side effects unless they carefully monitor their fat intake. Allí works by blocking fat absorption. Up to 25 percent of fat ingested is released through the bowels. A diet high in fat produces more waste, which results in cramping and other unpleasant side effects, such as loose stools, too-frequent stools, uncontrollable bowel movements, or gas with an oily discharge. In fact, the manufacturer recommends that people carry an extra pair of pants with them in case of anal leakage. Critics maintain that the drug prevents the body from absorbing important nutrients. As with most diet drugs there is little known about long-term benefits or consequences of using diet pills for weight loss.

The use of diet pills is just one controversial diet strategy for achieving weight loss. The following chapters discuss such strategies as gastric bypass surgery, lifestyle changes, the Atkins diet, and yoga as alternatives to dieting. In addition to discussing weight-loss options, this book contains a list of suggestions for further reading to help the reader further explore the topic and list of organizations to contact for further information. The appendix titled "What You Should Know About Dieting" offers facts about obesity and dieting, including health risks, and the appendix "What You Should Do About Dieting" offers tips on how to determine if a diet is necessary and when it might be appropriate to take action. With all of these features, *Issues That Concern You: Dieting* is not only an excellent tool for research, but it can also be used as a first step to diet awareness. Investigating all of the available options is one step on the road to educating yourself before selecting a particular diet. As with all health choices, you should speak to your doctor before deciding to commit to a certain diet or before taking any weight-loss supplements.

ONE

It Is Not Necessary to Lose Weight to Be Healthy

Paul Campos interviewed by Rebecca Traister

> In her interview with Paul Campos, Rebecca Traister gets to the bottom of the myth that Americans must lose weight in order to be healthy. Campos states that experts in weight management are often unable to live up to the body sizes they espouse, and that this type of "anorexic thinking" has created an obsession with becoming thin. Campos tells Rebecca Traister that Americans are more interested in looking like thin celebrities than in becoming healthy. Campos maintains that increasing physical activity is vastly more important to one's health than dieting. Paul Campos is an author and a professor of law at the University of Colorado. Rebecca Traister is a staff writer for *Salon*.

Paul Campos, a professor of law at the University of Colorado, argues passionately that the idea that America is in the midst of an obesity epidemic is false. He says that we're willing to buy into the notion of a national fat emergency because the medical profession and the media feed us misleading information about the connections between weight and health risks such as hypertension, cancer and heart disease. Campos says that what the studies actually show—before they have been garbled by an "anorexic" media—is that improved health is possible with a moderate amount of increased physical activity, regardless of our weight. But that message gets lost in the fever-pitch of fad diets, ever-shrinking government definitions of what it means to be overweight, and cultural discrimination against people who fail to meet the unrealistic and unnecessary standards for slimness.

[Rebecca Traister of] *Salon* spoke with Campos from his Colorado home about Jennifer Aniston's body mass index, Dr. Phil's near-obesity, and how we should worry more about the increased weight of automobiles than our own extra pounds.

Media's Obsession with Weight

You're a lawyer. How did you get interested in the medical profession's obsession with weight loss?

I was speaking at a conference on the [former president Bill] Clinton impeachment and I started looking at the media coverage of the [Monica] Lewinsky scandal and was struck by how frequently the media referred to Monica Lewinsky's weight. I was particularly struck by the frequent use of the word "zaftig" [full-figured]. Then Andrew Morton's book *Monica's Story* came out, and I was just astonished to read about the forthcomingness of Monica about her weight anxieties and Bill's and [former Pentagon employee] Linda Tripp's. It turned out that the bulk of what Monica and Tripp talked about was weight! There was this tremendous opprobrium that fell on Monica and Bill and Hillary [Clinton] for not having superthin bodies. Hillary particularly was constantly upbraided for having thick calves. I'm not sure what she was supposed to do about her calves.

But then even more scandalous was what I discovered through talking to lots of sociologists and people involved in the research end of all this. I discovered the tremendously exaggerated quality of the claims about how obesity—as defined by government standards—was being regarded as an epidemic that has direct correlation to health. I discovered what I consider to be a large cultural hysteria about how we're on the verge of a public health calamity. And what is essentially a social, cultural and political

Body Mass Index Table

BMI	Normal						Overweight					Obese						
Height (inches)	19	20	21	22	23	24	25	26	27	28	29	30	31	32	33	34	35	36
58	91	96	100	105	110	115	119	124	129	134	138	143	148	153	158	162	167	172
59	94	99	104	109	114	119	124	128	133	138	143	148	153	158	163	168	173	178
60	97	102	107	112	118	123	128	133	138	143	148	153	158	163	168	174	179	184
61	100	106	111	116	122	127	132	137	143	148	153	158	164	169	174	180	185	190
62	104	109	115	120	126	131	136	142	147	153	158	164	169	175	180	186	191	196
63	107	113	118	124	130	135	141	146	152	158	163	169	175	180	186	191	197	203
64	110	116	122	128	134	140	145	151	157	163	169	174	180	186	192	197	204	209
65	114	120	126	132	138	144	150	156	162	168	174	180	186	192	198	204	210	216
66	118	124	130	136	142	148	155	161	167	173	179	186	192	198	204	210	216	223
67	121	127	134	140	146	153	159	166	172	178	185	191	198	204	211	217	223	230
68	125	131	138	144	151	158	164	171	177	184	190	197	203	210	216	223	230	236
69	128	135	142	149	155	162	169	176	182	189	196	203	209	216	223	230	236	243
70	132	139	146	153	160	167	174	181	188	195	202	209	216	222	229	236	243	250
71	136	143	150	157	165	172	179	186	193	200	208	215	222	229	236	243	250	257
72	140	147	154	162	169	177	184	191	199	206	213	221	228	235	242	250	258	265
73	144	151	159	166	174	182	189	197	204	212	219	227	235	242	250	257	265	272
74	148	155	163	171	179	186	194	202	210	218	225	233	241	249	256	264	272	280
75	152	160	168	176	184	192	200	208	216	224	232	240	248	256	264	272	279	287
76	156	164	172	180	189	197	205	213	221	230	238	246	254	263	271	279	287	295

BMI	Obese			Extremely Obese														
Height (inches)	37	38	39	40	41	42	43	44	45	46	47	48	49	50	51	52	53	54
58	177	181	186	191	196	201	205	210	215	220	224	229	234	239	244	248	253	258
59	183	188	193	198	203	208	212	217	222	227	232	237	242	247	252	257	262	267
60	189	194	199	204	209	215	220	225	230	235	240	245	250	255	261	266	271	276
61	195	201	206	211	217	222	227	232	238	243	248	254	259	264	269	275	280	285
62	202	207	213	218	224	229	235	240	246	251	256	262	267	273	278	284	289	295
63	208	214	220	225	231	237	242	248	254	259	265	270	278	282	287	293	299	304
64	215	221	227	232	238	244	250	256	262	267	273	279	285	291	296	302	308	314
65	222	228	234	240	246	252	258	264	270	276	282	288	294	300	306	312	318	324
66	229	235	241	247	253	260	266	272	278	284	291	297	303	309	315	322	328	334
67	236	242	249	255	261	268	274	280	287	293	299	306	312	319	325	331	338	344
68	243	249	256	262	269	276	282	289	295	302	308	315	322	328	335	341	348	354
69	250	257	263	270	277	284	291	297	304	311	318	324	331	338	345	351	358	365
70	257	264	271	278	285	292	299	306	313	320	327	334	341	348	355	362	369	376
71	265	272	279	286	293	301	308	315	322	329	338	343	351	358	365	372	379	386
72	272	279	287	294	302	309	316	324	331	338	346	353	361	368	375	383	390	397
73	280	288	295	302	310	318	325	333	340	348	355	363	371	378	386	393	401	408
74	287	295	303	311	319	326	334	342	350	358	365	373	381	389	396	404	412	420
75	295	303	311	319	327	335	343	351	359	367	375	383	391	399	407	415	423	431
76	304	312	320	328	336	344	353	361	369	377	385	394	402	410	418	426	435	443

Taken from: www.fda.gov

concern has been transformed into a medical issue. And that ridiculous notion ends up being transmuted into the claim that it's only doctors who can be approved to speak authoritatively on it. And not just doctors—weight-loss doctors, who run weight-loss clinics and are benefiting from the hysteria.

Do you base your argument on what you found in studies, or have you also reported out this hysteria by talking to people in the weight-loss field?

I started out by reading studies and again and again ran into the same phenomenon: There was this disjunctive experience of reading the data and not being able to understand how conclusions about the correlation between weight and health stemmed from this data. I soon found people who were willing to say flat-out, "The reason you're having that experience is because those conclusions don't flow from that data." I asked a very prominent epidemiologist at the CDC. [Centers for Disease Control and Prevention] about the latest study that came out in March [2004], claiming that 400,000 deaths a year are a result of poor diet and a lack of activity level. I asked her how accurate that number was, and off the record—because she wants to keep her job—she said, "I think it's pretty accurate with a margin of error plus or minus 400,000 deaths a year."

The whole thing makes as much sense as *Reefer Madness* [a propaganda film about the dangers of smoking marijuana] or hysteria over satanic ritual abuse in our day-care centers. . . . Nevertheless, if they see something about an obesity epidemic on the front page of the *New York Times* and you ask them to consider the possibility that it's not true, they'll say how can you possibly question it when the NIH [National Institutes of Health] and CDC are telling you that it's true?

Obesity and Health

What is your reaction to the commonly held belief that there is a direct connection between obesity and ill health?

Something which ought to cause tremendous skepticism but hasn't is when you hear there is an epidemic of obesity in the U.S. According to official government standards, you're overweight if your BMI [body mass index] is over 25, which is 64.5 percent of the population on the basis of available data. Then there are the people at Harvard Medical School who think everyone should have a BMI of under 22 when 80 percent of the population is at 22 or higher. So according to all of them, the large majority of the population weighs too much. But there should be suspicion about the claim that there is a strong causal link between heart disease, hypertension, cancer—and weight. Because these diseases are less prevalent and less fatal than they were even recently. Cancer rates continue to fall. Americans are much healthier now and have a longer life expectancy than they ever had before. . . .

But isn't the idea of physical fitness—walking a half-hour a day—related to losing weight?

The evidence is very powerful that improved health among people who go from being sedentary to active is not due to weight loss, because for most people, increased physical activity does not produce significant long-term weight loss. And people who lose a lot of weight don't get any benefit over people who lose a little weight, so the benefit of weight loss by itself is medically nonexistent. But the good news is you don't have to become thinner to enjoy significantly improved health.

An Impossible Expectation

And you argue that the people telling us that we can get thinner aren't necessarily living by their own imposed guidelines?

I was at this *Time*/ABC obesity summit three weeks ago [June 2004] and [Secretary of Health and Human Services] Tommy Thompson is talking about how terrible this epidemic of obesity is—and he's not a slim guy. He's definitely obese by the standards he wants to impose. I was the lone dissenter, and there are tons of people out there questioning the war on obesity but they didn't invite any of them. They invited only the pain in the ass lawyer

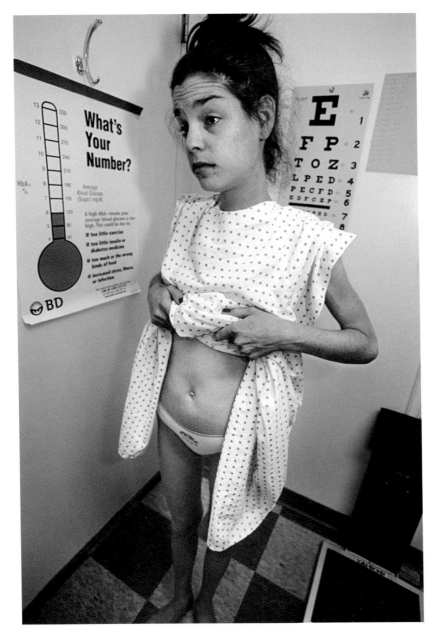

Teenagers are especially susceptible to pressure to lose weight from their peers and the media.

who's more easy to dismiss, because I'm not a medical professional. But one of the things I said is that all these people—most of them men—are overweight, or even obese by their own definitions.

I've really reached a wall of ideological incomprehension: How is it that people whose own bodies literally embody a refutation of their claim can keep getting up and haranguing us for being obese? What would people say if Tommy Thompson got up and lit up a big old fatty and then told all of us how terrible marijuana is? I assume people would say that doesn't seem to make a lot of sense! But literally no one ever says, "Well, wait a second, Mr. Secretary . . . how much do you weigh?" A central component of the whole obesity myth is that people could weigh significantly less if they wanted to, but these people at the forefront of the war on fat don't. . . .

What do you mean when you refer to people like [Harvard professor of epidemiology and nutrition Walter] Willet as anorexic?

I think these people have an anorexic ideation, to use a technical term. That means that their mind frame is similar to that of a person who is diagnosed as anorexic. One of the things that's true in this country is that the same kind of ideation—the same perceptual tendencies, same ideological orientation toward issues of weight—are found among many, many more people than the number of people who are technically diagnosed as having an eating disorder.

The line between having an eating disorder and eating-disordered thinking is very fuzzy. If you're obsessed with being thin, if you have major control issues, if you're obsessed with the idea that fat is bad and thin is good, if you place foods in good and bad categories, if you have an unrealistic body image and you think of yourself as fat—all that stuff is classic eating-disordered ideation. It's so normalized now that people don't even notice it.

What's happening is the institutionalization of this kind of ideation in the form of these government standards. I am not trying to be provocative here—this is what I actually think. Policies on this issue are strongly influenced by anorexic ideation. The NIH, the surgeon general, the official government public health agencies—in terms of definitions, in terms of advice about what people should be striving to achieve, in terms of the demonization, and the pathologizing of most of the range of normal body mass variation—they have turned most human bodies into diseased bodies by coming up with this very bizarre notion of what constitutes a normal body.

The Impact of Celebrity

How much of the obsession with weight loss has to do with people wanting to be healthier and how much has to do with people wanting to look like Jennifer Aniston?

There is overwhelming evidence that the latter consideration is vastly more important to people. As for Jennifer Aniston, she has a BMI of 18.3. Her [ex-]husband—the hunky Brad Pitt—has a BMI of 27.5. For Jennifer Aniston to have the same BMI index as her [ex-]husband she'd have to weight about 55 pounds more than she does now. That highlights the extent to which we put a premium on extreme slenderness as the sexually desirable ideal for women. Brad Pitt could be fairly described as a large individual. He appears to be in excellent shape. Largeness in men is considered quite desirable while extreme slenderness is what's supposed to be sexually attractive in women.

Wait. How do you know Jennifer Aniston and Brad Pitt's BMIs?

You can look up their height and weight on the Internet. And by the way, Jennifer Aniston is not extremely slender for a female celebrity, when you compare her to Gwyneth [Paltrow] or Madonna who have BMIs of 16. Dr. Phil's BMI is 29.5. He's almost obese! I just discovered that he's 6-foot-4 and weighs 240. He's way at the very top of the overweight range and that's Dr. Phil—America's big weight-loss guru.

Atkins Dieters Regain Weight

So what is your gut reaction if I mention the word "Atkins"?

My reaction is that [master showman and promoter] P.T. Barnum [of Ringling Brothers and Barnum & Bailey Circus] is spinning in his grave because he can't get in on this stuff.

It's safe to say that there is no more thoroughly investigated question in medicine than what happens when people restrict caloric intake for purposes of reducing weight: They lose the weight and gain it back again. It is absolutely amazing how impervious to evidence people are on these questions. It would be absurd at this point to ask whether cigarette smoking causes lung cancer. It's been investigated. Yes. It does. What happens if you have 100 people on Atkins is 95 of them one year later weigh as much or more than they did when they started. But there is something worse about Atkins, because low-carb dieting cuts aerobic endurance and since fitness level is vastly more important to health than weight, a diet that cuts fitness levels is perverse.

TWO

Most Americans Need to Lose Weight

Linda Bren

Linda Bren writes that according to the Centers for Disease Control and Prevention, more than 60 percent of Americans are overweight. She discusses small steps people can take to lose weight and cut health risks associated with obesity, and points out that there are four common factors among those who have lost weight and who have been able to keep it off. Bren also outlines important weight loss tools, such as setting goals, changing eating habits, watching calories, and exercising daily. Bren supplies her readers with an explanation of the body mass index and how it can be used to find out what is considered a healthy weight for adults. Linda Bren is a staff writer for the *FDA Consumer Magazine*.

Americans are getting fatter. We're putting on the pounds at an alarmingly rapid rate. And we're sacrificing our health for the sake of super-sized portions, biggie drinks, and two-for-one value meals, obesity researchers say.

More than 60 percent of U.S. adults are overweight, according to the Centers for Disease Control and Prevention (CDC). And about 15 percent of children and adolescents ages 6 to 19 are overweight.

Linda Bren, "Losing Weight: Start by Counting Calories," *FDA Consumer Magazine*, January–February 2002. Reproduced by permission.

Poor diet and physical inactivity account for more than 400,000 premature deaths each year in the United States, second only to deaths related to smoking, says the CDC. People who are overweight or obese are more likely to develop heart disease, stroke, high blood pressure, diabetes, gallbladder disease, and joint pain caused by excess uric acid (gout). Excess weight can also cause interrupted breathing during sleep (sleep apnea) and wearing away of the joints (osteoarthritis). Carrying extra weight means carrying an extra risk for certain types of cancer, including endometrial, breast, prostate, and colon cancer.

But there is hope for overweight Americans. They can take small, achievable steps to improve their health and reverse the obesity epidemic. This message is the cornerstone of a national education campaign announced in March 2004 by the Department of Health and Human Services (HHS).

As part of HHS' renewed efforts to combat obesity, the Food and Drug Administration's [FDA] Obesity Working Group released its Calories Count report in March 2004, highlighting actions that the agency will work toward to help consumers make smart choices about their diet. These actions include strengthening food labeling, educating consumers about maintaining a healthy diet and weight, and encouraging restaurants to provide calorie and nutrition information. Also included are increased enforcement to ensure food labels accurately portray serving size and strengthened scientific research aimed at reducing obesity and developing foods that are healthier and lower in calories.

Are You Overweight?

Overweight refers to an excess of body weight, but not necessarily body fat. Obesity means an excessively high proportion of body fat. Health professionals use a measurement called body mass index (BMI) to classify an adult's weight as healthy, overweight, or obese. BMI describes body weight relative to height and is correlated with total body fat content in most adults.

To get your approximate BMI, multiply your weight in pounds by 703, then divide the result by your height in inches, and divide

MyPyramid, launched in 2005, is one of many weight-management tools available to everyone.

that result by your height in inches a second time. (Or you can use the interactive BMI calculator at www.nhlbisupport.com/bmi/bmicalc.htm.)

A BMI from 18.5 up to 25 is considered in the healthy range, from 25 up to 30 is overweight, and 30 or higher is obese. Generally, the higher a person's BMI, the greater the risk for health problems, according to the National Heart, Lung and Blood Institute (NHLBI). However, there are some exceptions. For example, very muscular people, like body builders, may have a BMI greater than 25 or even 30, but this reflects increased muscle rather than fat. "It is excess body fat that leads to the health problems such as type 2 diabetes, high blood pressure, and high cholesterol," says Eric Colman, M.D., of the FDA's Division of Metabolic and Endocrine Drug Products.

In addition to a high BMI, having excess abdominal body fat is a health risk. Men with a waist of more than 40 inches around and women with a waist of 35 inches or more are at risk for health problems.

Obesity, once thought by many to be a moral failing, is now often classified as a disease. The NHLBI calls it a complex chronic disease involving social, behavioral, cultural, physiological, metabolic, and genetic factors. Although experts may have different theories on how and why people become overweight, they generally agree that the key to losing weight is a simple message: Eat less and move more. Your body needs to burn more calories than you take in. . . .

Successful "Losers"

Although many people who lose weight may eventually gain it back, it's a myth that this happens to everyone, says Rena Wing, Ph.D., a professor of psychiatry at Brown Medical School in Providence, R.I. Wing, the co-developer of a research study known as the National Weight Control Registry, has worked to deflate this myth.

Tucked away in the registry's database is information about the weight-control behaviors of more than 3,000 American adults who have lost an average of 60 pounds and have kept it off for an average of six years.

How Do They Do It?

These successful weight losers report four common behaviors, says Wing. They eat a low-calorie, low-fat diet, they monitor themselves by weighing in frequently, they are very physically active, and they eat breakfast. Eating breakfast every day is contrary to the typical pattern for the average overweight person who is trying to diet, says Wing. "They get up in the morning and say 'I'm going to start my diet today,' and they eat little or no breakfast and a light lunch. Then they get hungry and consume most of their calories late in the day. Successful weight losers have managed to change this pattern."

Six years after their weight loss, most of the registry's successful losers still report eating a low-calorie, low-fat diet. They also exercise for about an hour or more a day, expending about 2,800 calories per week on a variety of activities.

Wing also reports that more than 70 percent of the registry's weight losers became overweight before age 18. . . .

Setting a Goal

The first step to weight loss is setting a realistic goal. By using a BMI chart and consulting with your health care provider, you can determine what is a healthy weight for you.

Studies show that you can improve your health with just a small amount of weight loss. "We know that physical activity in combination with reduced calorie consumption can lead to the 5 to 10 percent weight loss necessary to achieve remission of the obesity-associated complications," says William Dietz, M.D., Ph.D., director of the Division of Nutrition and Physical Activity at the CDC. "Even these moderate weight losses can improve blood pressure and help control diabetes and high cholesterol in obese or overweight adults."

To reach your goal safely, plan to lose weight gradually. A weight loss of one-half to two pounds a week is usually safe, according to the Dietary Guidelines for Americans 2000. This can be achieved by decreasing the calories eaten or increasing the calories used by 250 to 1,000 calories per day, depending on current calorie intake. (Some people with serious health problems due to obesity may lose weight more rapidly under a doctor's supervision.) If you plan to lose more than 15 to 20 pounds, have any health problems, or take medication on a regular basis, see your health care professional before you begin a weight-loss program.

Changing Eating Habits

Dieting may conjure up visions of eating little but lettuce and sprouts—but you can enjoy all foods as part of a healthy diet as long as you don't overdo it. To be successful at losing weight, you need to change your lifestyle—not just go on a diet, experts say. This requires cutting back on the number of calories you eat by eating smaller amounts of foods and choosing foods lower in calories. It also means being more physically active.

Consider limiting portion sizes, especially of foods high in calories, such as cookies, cakes and other sweets; fried foods, like fried chicken and french fries; and fats, oils, and spreads. Reducing dietary fat alone—without reducing calories—will not produce weight loss, according to the NHLBI's guidelines on treating overweight and obesity in adults.

Use the Food Guide Pyramid developed by the U.S. Department of Agriculture and HHS to help you choose a healthful assortment of foods. Include bright-colored (red, yellow, green, and orange) vegetables and fruits, grains (especially whole grains), low-fat or fat-free milk, and fish, lean meat, poultry, or beans. Choose foods naturally high in fiber, such as fruits, vegetables, legumes (such as beans and lentils), and whole grains. The high fiber content of many of these foods may help you to feel full with fewer calories. To be sure that a food is whole grain, check the ingredient list on the food label—the first ingredient should be whole wheat or whole grain.

All calorie sources are not created equal. Carbohydrate and protein have about four calories per gram, but all fats, including oils like olive and canola oil, have more than twice that amount (nine calories per gram).

Keep your intake of saturated fat, trans fat, and cholesterol as low as possible. All of these fats raise LDL (or "bad cholesterol"), which increases your risk for coronary heart disease. Foods high in saturated fats include high-fat dairy products (like cheese, whole milk, cream, butter, and regular ice cream), fatty fresh and processed meats, the skin and fat of poultry, lard, palm oil, and coconut oil. Trans fat can often be found in processed foods made with partially hydrogenated vegetable oils such as vegetable

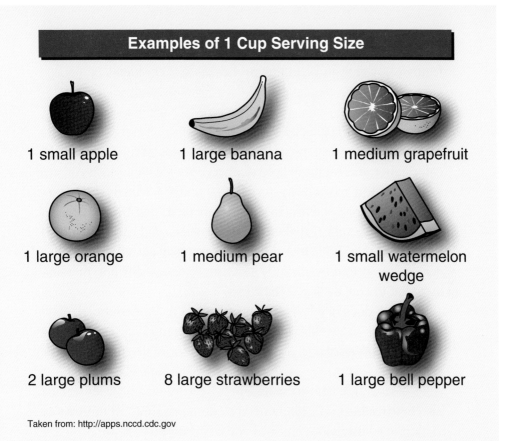

Examples of 1 Cup Serving Size

1 small apple

1 large banana

1 medium grapefruit

1 large orange

1 medium pear

1 small watermelon wedge

2 large plums

8 large strawberries

1 large bell pepper

Taken from: http://apps.nccd.cdc.gov

shortenings, some margarines (for example, stick margarines that are hard), crackers, cookies, candies, snack foods, fried foods and baked goods. . . .

Limit your use of beverages and foods that are high in added sugars—whose added to foods in processing or preparation, not the naturally occurring sugars in foods such as fruit or milk. Foods high in added sugars provide calories, but may have few of the other beneficial nutrients, such as fiber, vitamins, and minerals, that your body needs. A food high in added sugars will list a sugar as the first or second ingredient on the ingredient list. Some examples of added sugars are corn syrup, high fructose corn syrup, maltose, dextrose, honey, fruit juice concentrates, and maple syrup. In the United States, foods high in added sugars include non-diet soft drinks, sweetened beverages, including teas, fruit drinks, and fruitades, sweets and candies, and cakes and cookies. . . .

Increasing Physical Activity

Most health experts recommend a combination of a reduced-calorie diet and increased physical activity for weight loss.

In addition to helping to control weight, physical activity decreases the risk of dying from coronary heart disease and reduces the risk of developing diabetes, hypertension, and certain cancers. Researchers also have found that daily physical activity may help a person lose weight by partially lessening the slow-down in metabolism that occurs during weight loss.

Exercise does not have to be strenuous to be beneficial. And some studies show that short sessions of exercise several times a day are just as effective at burning calories and improving health as one long session.

To lose weight and to maintain a healthy weight after weight loss, many adults will likely need to do more than 30 minutes of moderate to intensive physical activity daily.

THREE

Gastric Bypass Surgery Is a Dangerous Dieting Trend for Teenagers

Helen Cordes

In the following article, Helen Cordes discusses the fact that the number of obese teenagers in America who are turning to gastric bypass surgery to lose weight has increased significantly in the last decade. According to Cordes, complications resulting from bariatric surgeries are on the rise as more unqualified surgeons opt to perform these risky procedures because the hefty price tag to patients means big profits for the doctors. Cordes points out that teenagers' bodies are not yet fully developed, and so malnutrition issues can be common after having the surgery. In addition to vitamin deficiencies, Cordes notes teens are often not emotionally mature enough to make the life changes necessary to ensure the surgery will not have to be performed again. Cordes also discusses risks such as infection, blot clots, and even death. Helen Cordes is a Journalism Fellow in Child and Family Policy through the University of Maryland.

Obese teens are a thriving slice of the dramatic rise in gastric bypass surgeries that soared from 16,200 in 1992 to an estimated 140,000 in 2004. Over 1,000 teens had surgeries last year

[2004], estimates Dr. Thomas Inge, director of the Comprehensive Weight Management Center at Cincinnati Children's Hospital.

The idea of a kid as young as 13 undergoing permanent stomach surgery sounds shocking to many. But surgery advocates such as Dr. Richard Atkinson, president of the American Obesity Association, defend the choice as a necessity: "Statistically speaking, obesity prevention and dieting simply hasn't worked."

American children lead the world's ranks in obesity, with 15 percent obese and another 30 percent overweight. Some 250,000 teens are at least 100 pounds overweight, a guideline often used for adult surgery criteria.

"The best way to lose weight is to have your stomach stapled...to your upper lip."

Kids as young as elementary school are developing the first stages of diabetes, heart disease, osteoarthritis, liver dysfunction and other illnesses that are typically paired with obesity. "We don't think of surgery as a weight-loss option," says Dr. Joey Skelton, director of the weight management program at the Children's Hospital of Wisconsin. "It's a last-ditch effort to address illness."

The teen surgery rise "is very appropriate," says Atkinson. "For the morbidly obese, nothing is anywhere near as effective." And when the weight stays off, patients who had diabetes or hypertension can sometimes reduce or eliminate medications.

But if many more teens head for the operating table, critics fear that they'll be subject to the same disturbing trends affecting the thousands of adults who have had surgery. The rate of complications and death from the procedure has edged up, as inexperienced surgeons flock to an industry valued at an annual $3 billion. Many patients regain some or all of their weight, and need re-operations.

And the long-term effects on kids "are a huge unknown," says Dr. Paul Ernsberger, associate professor of nutrition at Case Western Reserve University. Ernsberger and other critics worry about the eventual effects on brain, bone and muscle growth and health when a major source of nutrient absorption is bypassed during the teen years. "What will kids be experiencing 20 or 40 or 60 years from now?" Ernsberger wonders.

Weight Loss Surgery Is Big Business

For now, weight-loss surgery is a hot property, pushed by several potent factors. Marketing is at a fever pitch. Consumer demand is very high, with many hospitals booked months in advance with adults and teens, and insurers inundated by coverage requests. The ranks of the American Society of Bariatric Surgeons have swelled from 168 in 1993 to 860 in 2003, and critics complain that many hang out their shingle after a single weekend training.

While successful surgery scenarios—well trained, experienced surgeons with lots of hospital backup—have low complication and death rates, other situations can produce tragic results. Houston attorney Richard Mitloff represents 28 surgery patients who got their surgeries at facilities owned by a major Texas hospital chain.

"They marketed the surgery very aggressively," Mitloff charges. "They'd pay the airfare for patients, bring them in by limo, with an elaborate last meal before the surgery." After the surgeries, four patients died, and the others experienced major infections, stomach leakages, and other complications requiring more surgeries and leaving permanent injuries.

"Surgery can be very beneficial in the right circumstances," says Mitloff. "But this is a very lucrative business with procedures getting $30,000 to $40,000 each. A number of hospitals see nothing but dollar signs." . . .

Risk Factors

There's no question that for a teen or adult with plenty of motivation, surgery can work. [Charlie] Fabrikant is a best-case scenario: Having seen his mother lose weight with surgery, "I saw up close exactly what kinds of diet and exercise changes I'd have to make to keep the weight off," he says. Thus far, he's content with foregoing typical teen staples such as soda and pizza—foods high in fat and sugar, that can sometimes cause "dumping" symptoms of vomiting and diarrhea in many who've received surgery.

But best-case scenarios are not the norm. Despite reassuring industry statistics that typically put the death rate at 0.5 percent, risks are significant and can show up for years afterward. One study of 3,000 surgeries found a mortality rate of 5 percent with inexperienced surgeons, and analyses by the NIH [National Institutes of Health] and other agencies report that some 25 percent of patients suffer serious complications such as blood clots, infections, hernias, gastrointestinal leaks and bowel obstruction.

"Bariatric surgeries can be performed with reasonably low risks," says Livingston, who has performed thousands of them. "But the data doesn't always include problems that show up later."

He's concerned about reports of a 20–30 percent rate of major complications in California patients soon to be published; an

August [2005] report from a Pennsylvania health agency found that 39 percent of the nearly 7,000 surgery patients in 2003 required re-hospitalization.

Many patients are unable to stick to a radically different eating regimen and needed exercise, and all or part of the weight is regained in anywhere from 25 percent to the majority of cases, according to several studies. "Revisions"—surgeries redone because the patient stretches out the stomach pocket by falling back into old eating patterns—are common and even riskier.

Malnutrition Issues Are Common After Surgery

Like adults, teens who lose weight through surgery do find illness symptoms diminished. But while surgery guidelines call for waiting until growth has nearly stopped—typically the age of 13 for girls and 15 for boys—malnutrition issues are routine.

"Kids are supposed to take vitamins every day, but that can't replace everything a fully functioning stomach provides," says Ernsberger. He's concerned about widespread anemia and vitamin deficiencies that cause hair loss, nerve damage, and formerly obscure conditions such as beriberi [a nervous system ailment caused by a Vitamin B1 deficiency]. He worries that kids will get more infections and food poisoning because surgeries cut down the bacteria-killing role of stomach acid.

As for the surgery's potential to reduce disease? "We can treat kids with medications for diseases as they may appear—or not, if health changes are made—rather than have them undergo a permanent, life-altering surgery at a young age," says Ernsberger.

And can kids maintain the lifestyle changes needed to stay healthy and maintain weight loss? "I've evaluated a lot of kids and only found one I thought was mature enough to handle something as permanent as a surgery," says Livingston. "Most kids are not emotionally ready to make life-long changes."

One study showed fewer than 15 percent of teens followed their vitamin and calcium recommendations, and other studies show poor teen adherence to eating and exercise recommendations as well.

These downsides make some question whether surgery can live up to its healthcare cost-cutting potential. "I'm not sure it reduces costs, when the cost of complications are included," says Livingston. A Swedish study showed surgery patients still incurred higher costs than equally obese counterparts after six years, with reduced costs for diabetes and heart problems but increased costs for anemia and gastrointestinal disorders. . . .

The hazards of gastric bypass surgery can be life threatening and even deadly in some situations.

Lose It, Keep It Off

Kids can, of course, lose even large amounts of weight through healthy eating and exercise. Adults do it: one Maine elementary school teacher dropped from 763 pounds to 279 by eating better and moving more over a three-year period. And National Weight Loss Registry members—now numbering over 4,000—lost an average 66 pounds and kept it off for five years with an improved diet and increased exercise.

Traditional weight loss is a very difficult challenge for obese kids, says Noel Gonzalez, a counselor to obese kids at Texas Children's Hospital. "Our kids can barely walk a few blocks at a very slow pace, their feet and legs hurt, and they're embarrassed to be seen outside because they get teased so much," he notes. Kids can easily feel defeated, he notes—it's hard to get excited over a few lost pounds when there's 200 more to go.

But many who work with obese children insist that significant weight loss can happen with the proper support.

"The money that would be spent on surgery could go a long way to support comprehensive weight management programs for kids and their families," says Dr. Sarah Barlow, a childhood obesity specialist and pediatrics professor at St. Louis University School of Medicine. With one such eight-month program, a third of the kids reached and maintained normal weight in a 10-year follow-up study, she notes.

Will the future include more funding and insurance coverage for this solution? "It's certainly possible," says Barlow. With more programs, even if a child did end up with surgery, "at least that child would have learned healthy patterns that would help her maintain the weight loss."

FOUR

Lifestyle Changes Plus Medication Leads to Weight Loss

National Institute of Diabetes and Digestive and Kidney Diseases

In the following press release, the National Institute of Diabetes and Digestive and Kidney Diseases (NIDDK) announces that a recent study shows that weight-loss medications are more effective when used in combination with lifestyle changes. Study participants who received counseling, kept daily food and exercise logs, and took weight-loss medication lost twice as much weight as those who dieted using medication only. The NIDDK is one of the National Institutes of Health. NIDDK conducts research on diabetes, obesity, and other digestive diseases.

A new study shows that treatment with a lifestyle modification program of diet, exercise and behavioral therapy when used in combination with the weight loss medication . . . resulted in significantly greater weight loss among obese adults than treatment with the medication alone. The study, conducted by researchers from the University of Pennsylvania, appears in the November 17, 2005 issue of the *New England Journal of Medicine* and was supported by the National Institute of Diabetes and Digestive and Kidney Diseases (NIDDK), one of the National Institutes of Health (NIH).

National Institute of Diabetes and Digestive Kidney Diseases, "Lifestyle Modification Plus Medication More Effective than Medication Alone for Weight Loss in Obese Adults," *National Institutes of Health News*, November 16, 2005. Reproduced by permission.

"NIH is fighting the increasing problem of obesity in America by supporting research that will result in better treatments and therapies for weight loss and the prevention of obesity's associated diseases, such as type 2 diabetes, heart disease, and some forms of cancer," says NIH Director Elias A. Zerhouni, M.D.

"Lifestyle modification should be the first line of treatment for obesity," says Susan Yanovski, M.D., director of the Obesity and Eating Disorders Program for NIDDK, and author of an accompanying editorial in the journal. "But for obese adults who can't lose enough weight to improve their health, medication used as an adjunct can help."

"The take home message is that weight loss medications will be most effective when they are combined with a reduced calorie diet and increased physical activity," says Thomas A. Wadden, Ph.D., Professor of Psychology in the Department of Psychiatry at the University of Pennsylvania School of Medicine, and lead author of the study. "Weight loss medication used alone can produce some weight loss, but lifestyle modification treatment can help patients acquire skills to successfully make changes in their diet and physical activity."

The Study

A total of 224 obese adults aged 18 to 65 years participated in the one-year study. Participants were randomly assigned to one of four groups: 1. weight loss medication alone; 2. lifestyle modification alone; 3. weight loss medication plus lifestyle modification; and 4. weight-loss medication plus brief physician-mediated therapy. The researchers included the fourth treatment group to measure the effectiveness of weight-loss medication combined with brief lifestyle modification counseling delivered by primary care providers. The researchers looked at this type of therapy as a possible model for delivering lifestyle modification therapy in the setting of primary care practice.

Participants in the lifestyle modification therapy group attended a total of 30, 90-minute group meetings. During the meetings participants were instructed to complete and share weekly assign-

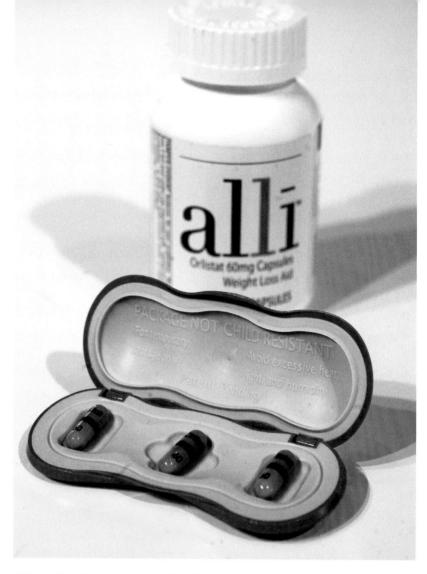

Diet pills alone may not be the solution to the obesity epidemic.

ments, which included keeping detailed daily food and physical activity records. Participants in the brief lifestyle modification counseling group met with primary care physicians eight times for 10 to 15 minute visits, where they were given homework assignments, which also included keeping daily food and activity records. Participants in the weight-loss medication therapy alone group also met with primary care physicians eight times for 10 to 15 minute visits, but were not instructed to keep food or activity records and were provided only general information on diet and exercise. Those participants in the combined therapy group received both the lifestyle modification therapy and the weight-loss medication. All groups were prescribed a 1200 to 1500 calorie diet and the same exercise plan.

After one year, patients in the weight-loss medication plus lifestyle group lost an average of more than 26 pounds—more than double the weight loss seen with medication alone (11 pounds). In addition, 73 percent of participants in the combined therapy group lost 5 percent or more of their initial body weight, compared to 56 percent of participants in the brief therapy plus weight-loss medication group, 53 percent of participants in the lifestyle modification alone group, and 42 percent of participants in the weight-loss medication alone therapy group. More than half or 52 percent of people in the combined therapy group lost 10 percent or more of their initial body weight compared to 29 percent of participants in the lifestyle modification alone group, 26 percent of participants in the brief therapy plus weight-loss medication group, and 26 percent of participants in the weight-loss medication alone group.

Food Logs Are Key to Success

Interestingly, those participants in the combined therapy group who were most successful were those who frequently recorded their food intake. Those participants with high adherence to food intake record keeping lost more than twice as much weight as those with low adherence (41.5 versus 17 pounds).

"Some people have questions about how they can do lifestyle modification," says Dr. Wadden. "I think that a first step is to complete daily food logs. Food records help people become aware of their eating patterns and identifying areas for improvement." Dr. Wadden adds that the second step to weight loss is to increase physical activity and one of the best ways to do that is to obtain a pedometer to count steps and gradually increase daily walking.

One limitation of the study is that it only included obese patients who were otherwise healthy and excluded obese patients with health problems possibly related to their obesity, such as

Daily Food and Activity Diary

	Monday	Tuesday	Wednesday	Thursday	Friday	Saturday	Sunday
Breakfast							
Lunch							
Dinner							
Activity							

GOALS: DIET   **PHYSICAL ACTIVITY**

BEHAVIOR

Taken from: National Heart, Lung and Blood Institute, www.nhlbi.gov

hypertension, cardiovascular disease, cerebrovascular disease, kidney disease, liver disease, and diabetes. Because many obese patients also have other conditions that can adversely affect their health, physicians should carefully monitor patients enrolled in weight-loss programs that include weight-loss medications.

The findings of the study are consistent with the NIH Obesity Clinical Guidelines, which recommend that weight loss medications be used in a supportive role to a comprehensive program of behavioral treatment, diet therapy, and increased physical activity. The NIH Obesity Clinical Guidelines state that the most successful strategies for weight loss include calorie reduction, increased physical activity, and behavioral therapy designed to improve eating and physical activity habits. The Guidelines also recommend that physicians prescribe a regimen of lifestyle therapy for at least six months before adding weight-loss medication to the regimen.

FIVE

Pharmaceutical Companies Market Dangerous Weight Loss Drugs to Obese Patients

Susan Kelleher

Susan Kelleher reports on the diet drug industry's far-reaching efforts to classify obesity as a disease and to promote dangerous medications for weight loss. According to Kelleher, the "fight against fat" began with the acceptance of the body mass index (BMI), standard for gauging obesity as well as indicating ideal weights for people based on the ratio of height to weight. Kelleher discusses the history of various diet drugs' acceptance by the Food and Drug Administration (FDA) and the politicking that went on to get them approved. She also presents the personal tragedy that Tami Melum suffered after taking the weight-loss drug Redux, which has since been banned by the FDA because of its link to heart valve damage. Susan Kelleher is a staff writer for the *Seattle Times*.

After being prescribed Redux and a drug combination known as "phen-fen," [Tami] Melum developed heart damage so severe that in 2002 surgeons had to cut open her chest and heart and install an artificial valve.

She is a tragic testament to what can go wrong in a system where the powerful pharmaceutical industry influences what constitutes a disease, who has it, and how it should be treated.

Before taking the drugs, Melum was overweight but healthy: Her cholesterol, blood pressure and blood sugar were all normal.

But that wasn't enough. By the mid-1990s, the medical establishment had changed its mind about people such as Melum. Some of the world's most prominent obesity experts, with backing from the drug industry and medical societies, defined obesity as a stand-alone "disease" that caused premature death and needed to be treated with drugs.

Suddenly, Tami Melum and millions like her were, by definition, sick.

In making obesity a disease, these experts helped create a billion-dollar market for the drugs that maimed Melum, killed hundreds, and damaged the hearts and lungs of tens of thousands.

The story of obesity shows how it became acceptable for doctors to risk killing or injuring people on the premise that it would save them from illnesses they might never get.

Body Mass Index Helped Fan the Flames of a Diet Craze

How did the fight against fat reach this point?

It started more than a decade ago as drug companies and their scientific consultants increasingly promoted using a Body Mass Index (BMI) of 30 as the trigger point for when someone should be treated for obesity, including being prescribed weight-loss drugs.

The BMI is a height-to-weight ratio that provides a rough estimate of body fat. Adapted from life-insurance company measures three decades ago, the BMI not only measures obesity but also sets ranges for "ideal weight" and "overweight."

With the dividing line between being overweight and obese set at a BMI of 30, a 5-foot-10 person would be obese once he weighed

209 pounds or more. About 30 percent of the nation's adults are estimated to be obese.

At the time the BMI standard was being promoted as a disease, only two prescription weight-loss drugs were available in the United States: phentermine, approved by the Food and Drug Administration (FDA) in 1959, and fenfluramine, sold as Pondimin, approved in 1973.

In the early 1990s, doctors began prescribing them together for weight loss, and a diet craze took off. The FDA had not signed off on the safety of the two being used together. This "off-label" use of phen-fen therefore carried unknown risks for patients and their prescribing doctors.

With the patent on Pondimin soon to expire, a drug company formulated a blend of molecules in the two drugs and created Redux, dexfenfluramine. Like phen-fen, it gave its users the feeling of being full.

With a new drug in the pipeline, the industry and its experts demonstrated a new urgency to define obesity as a chronic disease that should be treated with its own drug.

Defining Obesity

In May 1995, the National Institutes of Health (NIH) asked 24 experts to write guidelines for diagnosing and treating obesity. The expert panel officially defined obesity as a BMI of 30 or higher, and overweight as a BMI above 25 and below 30. The panel, which included the pharmacologist who created the phen-fen combo, was criticized for its ties to the drug and weight-loss industries.

In fall 1995, the FDA first took up the approval of Redux, owned at the time by Interneuron Pharmaceuticals. If approved, Redux would be the first new weight-loss drug in more than 20 years.

At the hearings, Interneuron presented data showing an obesity pandemic and said desperate measures were required to stop it from prematurely killing 300,000 Americans a year.

That controversial figure came from weight-loss experts and researchers who used epidemiological data from decades-old

Some prescription appetite suppressants have caused patients irreversible damage in the process of achieving their weight-loss goals.

health studies to build the case that excess body fat was a crisis more urgent than even AIDS. They estimated the economic cost in health care, including associated heart attacks, diabetes and other diseases, to be more than $60 billion a year.

The high costs and daunting death toll bolstered support for physicians to apply risky treatments to the obese, such as gastric bypass surgery, stomach banding or long-term courses of drugs that would be too dangerous to give to healthy people.

Although phen-fen and Redux were billed as lifesavers, they also were known to have fatal side effects in certain cases. . . .

Warnings Against the Use of Weight-Loss Drugs

The first outsider to publicly warn about Redux and heart damage was a medical technician at a Fargo, N.D., clinic. She noticed that echocardiograms of younger women, with no history of heart disease, showed severely damaged heart valves after taking the diet drugs. The doctor she worked for sent two dozen case files to the Mayo Clinic.

There at the clinic, cardiologists researched the matter and concluded that Redux and phen-fen were linked to heart-valve damage. The clinic announced this startling finding in summer 1997, and the FDA followed up with its own warning about the drugs to doctors, hospitals and the public.

Unaware, Melum took the drugs until September 1997, when a local pharmacist told her they had been pulled from the market. He told her she might be able to get her prescription filled elsewhere.

She tried without success but went on with her workouts.

In fact, Wyeth, which by then held the license to Redux, had pulled the drug from the market that month. It also stopped selling Pondimin, its brand-name fenfluramine, half of the phen-fen combo.

Melum said her doctor, Nadine Burrington in Mount Vernon, never contacted her after news broke of the potentially deadly side effects. Melum said the doctor eventually apologized and told her she had no idea the drugs would harm her.

Melum gave Burrington permission to discuss all aspects of her treatment with the *Seattle Times*. The doctor declined to be interviewed.

The first information Melum received about potential problems with her heart came in early 2001 in the form of an information packet Wyeth sent her. The mailing was part of its proposed legal settlement with hundreds of thousands of patients in a class-action lawsuit. Melum said she kept the information but ignored it until fall 2001. At a friend's urging, she applied for Wyeth's free testing, which discovered her valve damage.

Discovering Dangerous Side Effects

"The doctor told me if I had waited much longer, I would be a candidate for [a heart] transplant," Melum said.

In May 2002, a surgeon sawed through Melum's sternum, cut into her heart and replaced a valve that controls blood flow on the left side of her heart.

Within three weeks, she suffered an allergic reaction to the anesthesia and was hospitalized. Two days later, she was near death.

In emergency surgery at the University of Washington Medical Center, doctors inserted a tube in her chest and siphoned more than three quarts of fluid from her heart. Her husband, Glenn, watched and wondered how he was going to raise the boys by himself.

"I was standing there watching her just slip away from me," he said in an interview, looking to the ceiling to keep tears at bay.

The medical bills related to her surgeries topped $140,000.

Wyeth established a $3.7 billion trust fund for injured patients in 2000 as part of a proposed settlement and created a $1.2 billion supplemental fund for patients earlier this year [2005]. Wyeth said it expects to pay $21.1 billion to settle legal claims involving phen-fen and Redux.

Melum joined the lawsuit and settled her claim in December [2005]. After fees, she received $500,000. She now weighs more than when she started the drugs, has an eight-inch scar down her chest, and will have to take a daily blood thinner for life.

Weight-Loss Industry Works to Forge Treatment Guidelines

The industry lost a blockbuster obesity drug, but more were in development. In the years after the Redux fiasco, the weight-loss industry—doctors, nutritionists, weight-loss clinics, drug makers— supported efforts to keep obesity classified as a disease and successfully lobbied for insurance to cover its treatment.

Industry-sponsored obesity experts continued to support treatment guidelines for obesity that included prescribing drugs. Guidelines are essentially detailed steps for doctors in diagnosing and treating an ailment, including recommended drugs to prescribe.

The doctors who write guidelines are a powerful force in health care because their opinions become the blueprints that drug companies and medical societies use to teach doctors in the trenches how to prescribe newly approved drugs.

Many of the doctors who supported Redux, including [Dr. George] Bray of Louisiana State University and others, worked on the obesity guidelines for the NIH and the World Health Organization.

These experts ended up endorsing the notion that doctors should encourage obese patients to lose weight at almost any cost.

The guidelines also discussed the approval of future weight-loss drugs. New anti-obesity drugs should be approved if significant numbers of people taking them lost at least 5 percent of their body weight and kept it off, compared to those taking placebos.

The FDA agreed with that target.

The world's leading weight-loss experts also argued that weight-loss drugs should be given to marginally obese people who could not lose weight by other means and even to overweight people who had at least two other "at risk" conditions such as high cholesterol and elevated blood pressure.

Some of them argued that the FDA should approve new weight-loss drugs even if obese people lost only 7 pounds on them.

Critics of the guidelines, notably those not associated with the drug industry, argued that physical activity and fitness play a greater role in health than body fat. People can be fat and fit. . . .

More than 70 New Medicines in Development

Whether anyone is becoming healthier because of all the activity remains to be seen. What is clear is that people continue to gain weight, that governments are worried about what that could mean for the future of health-care spending, and that more weight-loss drugs will continue to hit the FDA pipeline.

Currently, two prescription weight-loss drugs are sold in the U.S., and more than 70 are in development.

Meanwhile, the lobbying arm of the drug industry, Pharmaceutical Research and Manufacturers of America (PhRMA), continues to press the FDA to allow overweight people to enroll in drug trials for new weight-loss drugs.

PhRMA also asked the FDA to stop referring to obese people as "relatively healthy" or "otherwise healthy." The industry group said such language "sends the wrong message" and does not reflect its view that obesity is a chronic disease requiring life-long intervention.

One person who will be paying close attention to the debate is Tami Melum.

Had she known then what she knows now, she never would have taken the risk that the drug-company experts minimized in their battle against fat.

"You may be a little overweight," she said, "but at least you have your health."

SIX

The Atkins Diet Is Dangerous and Ineffective

Michael Greger

In the following article, Michael Greger exposes the dangers associated with adherence to the Atkins Diet. Greger writes that medical authorities' research concludes that there are no known health benefits to the low-carbohydrate, high-protein, and fat-heavy diet and that such extreme dieting poses a multitude of health risks. According to Greger, researchers who compared four popular diets found that the Atkins Diet did not significantly lower insulin levels as it was designed to do and that carbohydrates are necessary for energy and overall well-being. Finally, Greger asserts that those on the Atkins Diet were not able to maintain their initial weight loss over time. Michael Greger is a physician, lecturer, and a member of the American College of Lifestyle Medicine.

When *Dr. Atkins Diet Revolution* was first published, the President of the American College of Nutrition said, "Of all the bizarre diets that have been proposed in the last 50 years, this is the most dangerous to the public if followed for any length of time."

Recommended Daily Carbohydrate Intake

Atkins Diet	
Phase I Induction	20 grams for 14 days
Phase II Ongoing Weight Loss (OWL)	25 grams – gradually increase by 5 grams per day

Taken from: www.atkins.com

Iowa State University Extension	
Body at Rest	130 grams
Athletes	250 grams

Taken from: Iowa State University Extension, Copyright 2006 Iowa State University Extension

Nutrition Experts Weigh-In

When the chief health officer for the State of Maryland was asked "What's wrong with the Atkins Diet?" He replied "What's wrong with . . . taking an overdose of sleeping pills? You are placing your body in jeopardy." He continued "Although you can lose weight on these nutritionally unsound diets, you do so at the risk of your health and even your life."

The Chair of Harvard's nutrition department went on record before a 1973 U.S. Senate Select Committee investigating fad diets: "The Atkins Diet is nonsense. . . . Any book that recommends, unlimited amounts of meat, butter, and eggs, as this one does, in my opinion is dangerous. The author who makes the suggestion is guilty of malpractice."

The Chair of the American Medical Association's [AMA] Council on Food and Nutrition testified before the Senate Subcommittee as to why the AMA felt they had to formally publish an official condemnation of the Atkins Diet: "A careful scientific appraisal was carried out by several council and staff members, aided by outside consultants. It became apparent that the [Atkins] diet as recommended poses a serious threat to health."

The warnings from medical authorities continue to this day. "People need to wake up to the reality," former U.S. Surgeon General C. Everett Koop writes, that the Atkins Diet is "unhealthy and can be dangerous."

The world's largest organization of food and nutrition professionals, calls the Atkins Diet "a nightmare of a diet." The official spokesperson of the American Dietetic Association [ADA] elaborated: "The Atkins Diet and its ilk—any eating regimen that encourages gorging on bacon, cream and butter while shunning apples, all in the name of weight loss—are a dietitian's nightmare." The ADA has been warning Americans about the potential hazards of the Atkins Diet for almost 30 years now. Atkins dismissed such criticism as "dietician talk". "My English sheepdog," Atkins once said, "will figure out nutrition before the dieticians do."

The problem for Atkins (and his sheepdog), though, is that the National Academy of Sciences, the most prestigious scientific body in the United States, agrees with the AMA and the ADA in opposing the Atkins Diet. So does the American Cancer Society; and the American Heart Association; and the Cleveland Clinic; and Johns Hopkins; and the American Kidney Fund; and the American College of Sports Medicine; and the National Institutes of Health.

In fact there does not seem to be a single major governmental or nonprofit medical, nutrition, or science-based organization in the world that supports the Atkins Diet. As a 2004 medical journal review concluded, the Atkins Diet "runs counter to all the current evidence-based dietary recommendations."

Assessing Low-Carb Diets

A 2003 review of Atkins "theories" in the *Journal of the American College of Nutrition* concluded: "When properly evaluated, the theories and arguments of popular low carbohydrate diet books . . . rely on poorly controlled, non-peer-reviewed studies, anecdotes and non-science rhetoric. This review illustrates the complexity of nutrition misinformation perpetrated by some popular press diet books. A closer look at the science behind the claims made for [these books] reveals nothing more than a modern twist on an antique food fad." . . .

Faulty Science

The entire theoretical framework of low carb diets, like Atkins and The Zone, hang upon the notion that insulin is the root of all evil and so to limit insulin release one needs to limit carbohydrate intake. Dr. Atkins, for example, has a chapter entitled "Insulin—The Hormone That Makes You Fat," *Protein Power* calls it the monster hormone, and the author of *The Zone Diet* calls insulin "the single most significant determinant of your weight."

What they overlook is that "protein- and fat-rich foods may induce substantial insulin secretion" as well. Research in which study subjects served as their own controls, for example, has shown that under fasting conditions a quarter pound of beef raises insulin levels in diabetics as much as a quarter pound of straight sugar.

Atkins' featured foods like cheese and beef elevated insulin levels higher than "dreaded" high-carbohydrate foods like pasta. A single burger's worth of beef, or three slices of cheddar, boosts insulin levels more than almost 2 cups of cooked pasta. In fact a study in the *American Journal of Clinical Nutrition* found that meat, compared to the amount of blood sugar it releases, seems to cause the most insulin secretion of any food tested.

Selective Science

Low carb advocates like Atkins seem to completely ignore these facts. Recent medical reviews have called Atkins' feel-good theories "factually flawed" and "at best half-truths." "In the scientific world, books like *The Zone Diet* are generally regarded as fiction," one reviewer wrote in the *Journal of the American College of Nutrition*. "The scientific literature is in opposition." In a medical journal article entitled "Food Fads and Fallacies," the Atkins Diet is referred to as a "'New wives' tale" with a "sprinkling of fallacies."

According to a 2003 article in the *Journal of the American Medical Association*, "Dr. Atkins and his colleagues selectively recite the literature" to support their claims. When researchers take the time to actually measure insulin levels, for instance, instead of just talking about them like Atkins does, they often find the opposite of what Atkins asserted.

A study done at Tufts [University], for example, presented at the 2003 American Heart Association convention, compared four popular diets for a year. They compared Weight Watchers, The Zone Diet, the Atkins Diet (almost no carbs), and the Ornish Diet (almost all carbs) for a year. The insulin levels of those instructed to go on the Ornish diet dropped 27%. Out of the four diets that were compared that year, Ornish's vegetarian diet was the only one to significantly lower the "Monster" "Hormone That Makes You Fat," even though that's supposedly what Atkins and The Zone diets were designed to do.

In another study researchers took over a hundred pairs of identical twins and found that the more fat they ate, the *higher* their resting insulin levels were. Even with the same genes, the study "showed a consistent pattern of higher fasting insulin levels with intake of high-fat, low carbohydrate diets."

Other studies show that a high (70–85%) carbohydrate diet (combined with walking an average of 15–30 minutes a day) not only can result in significant reductions in body weight, blood pressure, cholesterol and triglycerides, but significant drops in baseline insulin levels as well, exactly the opposite of what low carb pushers would predict. In just three weeks on a high (unrefined) carb vegetarian diet and a few minutes of daily walking, diabetics reduced the amount of insulin they needed and most of the pre-diabetics seemed cured of their insulin resistance. In general vegetarians may have half the insulin levels of nonvegetarians even at the same weight. . . .

Low Calorie Diet in Disguise

The Atkins Diet restricts calories by restricting choices. If all one did was eat Twinkies, one could lose weight (unless one were able to consistently force oneself to eat more than a dozen a day). But would one's overall health be better or worse for it? In essence, the Atkins Diet is not much different than the Twinkie Diet.

Americans get half of their energy from carbohydrates, so if people cut out half the food they eat, what they are left with is calorie restriction. Yes, one can eat unlimited amounts of fat on the Atkins Diet, but people typically can't stomach an extra two sticks of butter's worth a day to make up for the calorie deficit. Since so many foods are taboo, people end up eating less out of sheer boredom and lack of variety. As one obesity researcher put it, "If you're only allowed to shop in two aisles of the grocery store, does it matter which two they are?"

Yes, all the butter one can eat, but no bread to put it on. All the cream cheese, but no bagels. Sour cream, but no baked potato. Sandwich lunchmeat, but, of course, no sandwiches. All the pepperoni one can eat, but no pizza crust. Cheese, but no mac.

In later phases of the diet, with less carb restriction, Atkins throws in a thin wedge of cantaloupe—wrapped in ham, of course. Having all the mayonnaise one can eat only goes so far.

On the Atkins Diet one can eat steak, but no potatoes—and watch the gravy (it may have corn starch in it). All the shortening one can eat, just no making cookies with it. Eat all the burgers one wants; you just can't put them on buns, no fries—and "beware of ketchup."

Atkins described how to make cheeseburgers without the bun: "I put all the meat on the outside . . . put the cheese on the inside. . . . The cheese melts on the inside and never gets out."

Although his recipe for "hamburger fondue," combining burger meat, blue cheese, and butter, might top the cheeseburger recipe for heart disease risk, the prize would probably go to his recipe for "Swiss Snack," which consists of wrapping bacon strips around cubes of Swiss cheese and deep frying them in hot oil. The recipe, which supposedly serves one, calls for four strips of bacon and a quarter-pound of cheese. . . .

Atkins Comes in Last for Long-Term Weight Maintenance

Even if people can handle the side effects of the diet, there are no data to show that the initial rapid weight loss on the Atkins Diet

The Atkins diet is one of the most controversial weight-loss programs in today's culture.

can be maintained long term. Many of the studies on the Atkins Diet have lasted only a few days; the longest the Atkins Diet has ever been formally studied is one year.

There have been 4 such yearlong studies and not a single one showed significantly more weight lost at the end of the year on the Atkins Diet than on the control "low fat" diets. In the yearlong comparison of the Atkins Diet to Ornish's diet, Weight Watchers, and The Zone Diet, the Atkins Diet came in dead *last* in terms of weight lost at the end of the year. Ornish's vegetarian diet seemed to show the most weight loss. The Atkins website had no comment.

Noting that by the end of the year, half of the Atkins group had dropped out, and those who remained ended up an unimpressive 4% lighter, *Fat of The Land* author Michael Fumento commented, "do you really think any of them could sell a single book copy, much less as many as 15 million (for Atkins), by admitting to a 50 percent drop-out rate in one year with a mere five percent of weight loss among those left?" . . .

The only other two formal yearlong studies found that although the initial drop in weight on Atkins was more rapid, weight loss on the Atkins Diet reversed or stalled after 6 months. The longer people stay on the Atkins Diet, the worse they seemed to do. None of the four longest studies on the Atkins Diet showed a significant advantage over just the type of high carbohydrate diets Atkins blamed for making America fat.

Anyone can lose weight on a diet; the critical question is whether the weight loss can be maintained and at what cost. If low carb diets really did cure obesity, the original in 1864 [a diet in the book *Letter on Corpulence* by William Banting] would have eliminated the problem and no more diet revolutions would be necessary. Short-term weight loss is not the same thing as lifelong weight maintenance. . . .

SEVEN

The Atkins Diet Is the Answer to America's Obesity Epidemic

Gary Taubes

In the following article, Gary Taubes discusses changing professional opinions regarding the controversial high-protein, low-carbohydrate Atkins Diet. Taubes reports that America's rising numbers of obese persons have caused the medical community to take a second look at its long-standing recommendation of a low-fat, high-carbohydrate diet. Many have started to wonder if this traditionally recommended diet is actually making people fat. Ridiculed as a "quack," Dr. Atkins has maintained for thirty years that his diet works and researchers are now starting to pay attention. Taubes presents studies that show people not only lose weight on the Atkins Diet, but they lose more than people on low-fat, low-calorie diets. Gary Taubes is a reporter for the *Journal of Science* and author of *Bad Science: The Short Life and Weird Science of Cold Fusion.*

If the members of the American medical establishment were to have a collective find-yourself-standing-naked-in-Times-Square-type nightmare, this might be it. They spend 30 years ridiculing Robert Atkins, author of the phenomenally-best-selling *Dr. Atkins' Diet Revolution* and *Dr. Atkins' New Diet Revolution*, accusing the Manhattan doctor of quackery and fraud, only to discover that the unrepentant Atkins was right all along. Or maybe it's this: they find that their very own dietary recommendations—eat less fat and more carbohydrates—are the cause of the rampaging epidemic of obesity in America. Or, just possibly this: they find out both of the above are true.

When Atkins first published his *Diet Revolution* in 1972, Americans were just coming to terms with the proposition that fat—particularly the saturated fat of meat and dairy products—was the primary nutritional evil in the American diet. Atkins managed to sell millions of copies of a book promising that we would lose weight eating steak, eggs and butter to our heart's desire, because it was the carbohydrates, the pasta, rice, bagels and sugar, that caused obesity and even heart disease. Fat, he said, was harmless.

Atkins allowed his readers to eat "truly luxurious foods without limit," as he put it, "lobster with butter sauce, steak with béarnaise sauce . . . bacon cheeseburgers," but allowed no starches or refined carbohydrates, which means no sugars or anything made from flour. Atkins banned even fruit juices, and permitted only a modicum of vegetables, although the latter were negotiable as the diet progressed.

Atkins was by no means the first to get rich pushing a high-fat diet that restricted carbohydrates, but he popularized it to an extent that the American Medical Association [AMA] considered it a potential threat to our health. The AMA attacked Atkins's diet as a "bizarre regimen" that advocated "an unlimited intake of saturated fats and cholesterol-rich foods," and Atkins even had to defend his diet in Congressional hearings.

Carbohydrates Make Us Fat

Thirty years later, America has become weirdly polarized on the subject of weight. On the one hand, we've been told with almost religious certainty by everyone from the surgeon general on down, and we have come to believe with almost religious certainty, that obesity is caused by the excessive consumption of fat, and that if we eat less fat we will lose weight and live longer. On the other, we have the ever-resilient message of Atkins and decades' worth of best-selling diet books, including *The Zone, Sugar Busters* and *Protein Power* to name a few. All push some variation of what scientists would call the alternative hypothesis: it's not the fat that makes us fat, but the carbohydrates, and if we eat less carbo-hydrates we will lose weight and live longer.

The perversity of this alternative hypothesis is that it identi-fies the cause of obesity as precisely those refined carbohydrates at the base of the famous Food Guide Pyramid—the pasta, rice and bread—that we are told should be the staple of our healthy low-fat diet, and then on the sugar or corn syrup in the soft drinks, fruit juices and sports drinks that we have taken to consuming in quantity if for no other reason than that they are fat free and so appear intrinsically healthy. While the low-fat-is-good-health dogma represents reality as we have come to know it, and the government has spent hundreds of millions of dollars in research

Advocates for the Atkins diet point to studies that show how successful it can be in overweight people.

trying to prove its worth, the low-carbohydrate message has been relegated to the realm of unscientific fantasy.

Over the past five years, however, there has been a subtle shift in the scientific consensus. It used to be that even considering the possibility of the alternative hypothesis, let alone researching it, was tantamount to quackery by association. Now a small but growing minority of establishment researchers have come to take seriously what the low-carb-diet doctors have been saying all along. Walter Willett, chairman of the department of nutrition at the Harvard School of Public Health, may be the most visible proponent of testing this heretic hypothesis. Willett is the de facto spokesman of the longest-running, most comprehensive diet and health studies ever performed, which have already cost upward of $100 million and include data on nearly 300,000 individuals. Those data, says Willett, clearly contradict the low-fat-is-good-health message "and the idea that all fat is bad for you; the exclusive focus on adverse effects of fat may have contributed to the obesity epidemic."

Low-Fat Diets Cause People to Gain Weight

These researchers point out that there are plenty of reasons to suggest that the low-fat-is-good-health hypothesis has now effectively failed the test of time. In particular, that we are in the midst of an obesity epidemic that started around the early 1980's, and that this was coincident with the rise of the low-fat dogma. (Type 2 diabetes, the most common form of the disease, also rose significantly through this period.) They say that low-fat weight-loss diets have proved in clinical trials and real life to be dismal failures, and that on top of it all, the percentage of fat in the American diet has been decreasing for two decades. Our cholesterol levels have been declining, and we have been smoking less, and yet the incidence of heart disease has not declined as would be expected. "That is very disconcerting," Willett says. "It suggests that something else bad is happening."

The science behind the alternative hypothesis can be called Endocrinology 101, which is how it's referred to by David Ludwig, a researcher at Harvard Medical School who runs the pediatric obesity clinic at Children's Hospital Boston, and who prescribes his own version of a carbohydrate-restricted diet to his patients. Endocrinology 101 requires an understanding of how carbohydrates affect insulin and blood sugar and in turn fat metabolism and appetite. This is basic endocrinology, Ludwig says, which is the study of hormones, and it is still considered radical because the low-fat dietary wisdom emerged in the 1960's from researchers almost exclusively concerned with the effect of fat on cholesterol and heart disease. At the time, Endocrinology 101 was still underdeveloped, and so it was ignored. Now that this science is becoming clear, it has to fight a quarter century of anti-fat prejudice.

The alternative hypothesis also comes with an implication that is worth considering for a moment, because it's a whopper, and it may indeed be an obstacle to its acceptance. If the alternative hypothesis is right—still a big "if"—then it strongly suggests that the ongoing epidemic of obesity in America and elsewhere is not, as we are constantly told, due simply to a collective lack of will power and a failure to exercise. Rather it occurred, as Atkins has been saying (along with Barry Sears, author of *The Zone*), because the public health authorities told us unwittingly, but with the best of intentions, to eat precisely those foods that would make us fat, and we did. We ate more fat-free carbohydrates, which, in turn, made us hungrier and then heavier. Put simply, if the alternative hypothesis is right, then a low-fat diet is not by definition a healthy diet. In practice, such a diet cannot help being high in carbohydrates, and that can lead to obesity, and perhaps even heart disease. "For a large percentage of the population, perhaps 30 to 40 percent, low-fat diets are counterproductive," says Eleftheria Maratos-Flier, director of obesity research at Harvard's prestigious Joslin Diabetes Center. "They have the paradoxical effect of making people gain weight." . . .

The Atkins Diet Works

The 71-year-old Atkins, a graduate of Cornell medical school, says he first tried a very low carbohydrate diet in 1963 after reading about one in the *Journal of the American Medical Association*. He lost weight effortlessly, had his epiphany and turned a fledgling Manhattan cardiology practice into a thriving obesity clinic. He then alienated the entire medical community by telling his readers to eat as much fat and protein as they wanted, as long as they ate little to no carbohydrates. They would lose weight, he said, because they would keep their insulin down; they wouldn't be hungry; and they would have less resistance to burning their own fat. Atkins also noted that starches and sugar were harmful in any event because they raised triglyceride levels and that this was a greater risk factor for heart disease than cholesterol.

Atkins's diet is both the ultimate manifestation of the alternative hypothesis as well as the battleground on which the fat-versus-carbohydrates controversy is likely to be fought scientifically over the next few years. After insisting Atkins was a quack for three decades, obesity experts are now finding it difficult to ignore the copious anecdotal evidence that his diet does just what he has claimed. Take Albert Stunkard, for instance. Stunkard has been trying to treat obesity for half a century, but he told me he had his epiphany about Atkins and maybe about obesity as well just recently when he discovered that the chief of radiology in his hospital had lost 60 pounds on Atkins's diet. "Well, apparently all the young guys in the hospital are doing it," he said. "So we decided to do a study." When I asked Stunkard if he or any of his colleagues considered testing Atkins's diet 30 years ago, he said they hadn't because they thought Atkins was "a jerk" who was just out to make money: this "turned people off, and so nobody took him seriously enough to do what we're finally doing."

In fact, when the American Medical Association released its scathing critique of Atkins's diet in March 1973, it acknowledged that the diet probably worked, but expressed little interest in why. Through the 60's, this had been a subject of considerable research, with the conclusion that Atkins-like diets were low-calorie diets in disguise; that when you cut out pasta, bread and potatoes, you'll have a hard time eating enough meat, vegetables and cheese to replace the calories.

Ketosis Kick-Starts Weight Loss

That, however, raised the question of why such a low-calorie regimen would also suppress hunger, which Atkins insisted was the signature characteristic of the diet. One possibility was Endocrinology 101: that fat and protein make you sated and, lacking carbohydrates and the ensuing swings of blood sugar and insulin, you stay sated. The other possibility arose from the fact that Atkins's diet is "ketogenic." This means that insulin falls so low that you enter a state called ketosis, which is what happens during fasting and starvation. Your muscles and tissues burn body fat for energy, as does your brain in the form of fat molecules produced by the liver called ketones. Atkins saw ketosis as the obvious way to kick-start weight loss. He also liked to say that ketosis was so energizing that it was better than sex, which set him up for some ridicule. An inevitable criticism of Atkins's diet has been that ketosis is dangerous and to be avoided at all costs.

When I interviewed ketosis experts, however, they universally sided with Atkins, and suggested that maybe the medical community and the media confuse ketosis with ketoacidosis, a variant of ketosis that occurs in untreated diabetics and can be fatal. "Doctors are scared of ketosis," says Richard Veech, an NIH [National Institutes of Health] researcher who studied medicine at Harvard and then got his doctorate at Oxford University with the Nobel Laureate Hans Krebs. "They're always worried about diabetic ketoacidosis. But ketosis is a normal physiologic state. I would argue it is the normal state of man. It's not normal to have McDonald's and a delicatessen around every corner. It's normal to starve."

Simply put, ketosis is evolution's answer to the thrifty gene [hypothesis that certain ethnic groups are predisposed to obesity]. We may have evolved to efficiently store fat for times of famine, says Veech, but we also evolved ketosis to efficiently live off that fat when necessary. Rather than being poison, which is how the press often refers to ketones, they make the body run more efficiently and provide a backup fuel source for the brain. Veech calls ketones "magic" and has shown that both the heart and brain run 25 percent more efficiently on ketones than on blood sugar.

Testing the Atkins Diet

The bottom line is that for the better part of 30 years Atkins insisted his diet worked and was safe, Americans apparently tried it by the tens of millions, while nutritionists, physicians, public-health authorities and anyone concerned with heart disease insisted it could kill them, and expressed little or no desire to find out who was right. During that period, only two groups of U.S. researchers tested the diet, or at least published their results. In the early 70's, J.P. Flatt and Harvard's George Blackburn pioneered the "protein-sparing modified fast" to treat postsurgical patients, and they tested it on obese volunteers. Blackburn, who later became president of the American Society of Clinical Nutrition, describes his regime as "an Atkins diet without excess fat" and says he had to give it a fancy name or nobody would take him seriously. The diet was "lean meat, fish and fowl" supplemented by vitamins and minerals. "People loved it," Blackburn recalls. "Great weight loss. We couldn't run them off with a baseball bat." Blackburn successfully treated hundreds of obese patients over the next decade and published a series of papers that were ignored. When obese New Englanders turned to appetite-control drugs in the mid-80's, he says, he let it drop. He then applied to the NIH for a grant to do a clinical trial of popular diets but was rejected.

The second trial, published in September 1980, was done at the George Washington University Medical Center. Two dozen obese volunteers agreed to follow Atkins's diet for eight weeks and lost an average of 17 pounds each, with no apparent ill effects, although their L.D.L. cholesterol did go up. The researchers, led by John LaRosa, now president of the State University of New York Downstate Medical Center in Brooklyn, concluded that the 17-pound weight loss in eight weeks would likely have happened with any diet under "the novelty of trying something under experimental conditions" and never pursued it further.

Now researchers have finally decided that Atkins's diet and other low-carb diets have to be tested, and are doing so against traditional low-calorie-low-fat diets as recommended by the American Heart Association. To explain their motivation, they inevitably tell one of two stories: some, like Stunkard, told me that someone they knew—a patient, a friend, a fellow physician—lost considerable weight on Atkins's diet and, despite all their preconceptions to the contrary, kept it off. Others say they were frustrated with their inability to help their obese patients, looked into the low-carb diets and decided that Endocrinology 101 was compelling. "As a trained physician, I was trained to mock anything like the Atkins diet," says Linda Stern, an internist at the Philadelphia Veterans Administration Hospital, "but I put myself on the diet. I did great. And I thought maybe this is something I can offer my patients."

None of these studies have been financed by the NIH and none have yet been published. But the results have been reported at conferences—by researchers at Schneider Children's Hospital on Long Island, Duke University and the University of Cincinnati, and by Stern's group at the Philadelphia V.A. Hospital. And then there's the study Stunkard had mentioned, led by Gary Foster at the University of Pennsylvania, Sam Klein, director of the Center for Human Nutrition at Washington University in St. Louis, and Jim Hill, who runs the University of Colorado Center for Human Nutrition in Denver. The results of all five of these studies are remarkably consistent. Subjects on some form of the Atkins diet —whether overweight adolescents on the diet for 12 weeks as at Schneider, or obese adults averaging 295 pounds on the diet for six months, as at the Philadelphia V.A.—lost twice the weight as the subjects on the low-fat, low-calorie diets.

In all five studies, cholesterol levels improved similarly with both diets, but triglyceride levels were considerably lower with the Atkins diet. Though researchers are hesitant to agree with this, it does suggest that heart-disease risk could actually be reduced when fat is added back into the diet and starches and refined carbohydrates are removed. "I think when this stuff gets to be recognized," Stunkard says, "it's going to really shake up a lot of thinking about obesity and metabolism."

EIGHT

Practicing Yoga Is a Better Alternative to Dieting

Ingrid Cummings

> According to Ingrid Cummings, the practice of yoga encourages "mindful eating," which is an awareness of the number of calories a body needs to operate. Cummings writes that yoga also teaches how to intuitively know when to stop eating. Cummings states that being in touch with one's caloric needs prevents overeating and promotes healthy responses to challenging situations. She writes that the food industry does not make it easy for people to eat well or to have a healthy relationship with food, and that it, in fact, markets unhealthy eating habits and encourages using food in response to emotional upheaval. Cummings believes that yoga can help combat the food and diet industries' negative messages by teaching those who practice regularly how to eat with joy and to have compassion for oneself instead of self-loathing. Ingrid Cummings is a journalist and a producer and host of the radio show *Rubicon Salon*.

The [yoga] discipline's philosophy teaches you to make your meals from plant-based foods that form the foundation of the food pyramid—foods over which there's much less squabbling among nutrition experts. The physical practice deepens your

Ingrid Cummings, "Fear Factor," *Yoga Journal*, February 2006. Reproduced by permission.

awareness of your body, so you become more conscious of foods that bring a consistent sense of well-being—and those that make you feel bad after you eat them. Over time, practitioners often find themselves in a more comfortable and relaxed relationship with food. . . .

Scientists are now turning up demonstrable evidence of yoga's benefits in this area. A recent study from the Fred Hutchinson Cancer Research Center in Seattle found that middle-aged men and women who were overweight and practiced yoga at least once a week lost five pounds over a 10-year period. Their non-yogi counterparts gained eight pounds. Lead researcher Alan Kristal, a professor of epidemiology at the University of Washington School of Public Health and Community Medicine, believes the weight loss had more to do with an increase in mindfulness than in calories burned. "You learn to feel when you're full, and you don't like the feeling of overeating," he says. "You recognize anxiety and stress for what they are instead of trying to mask them with food."

Bianca Raffety can attest to this phenomenon. The 36-year-old Anusara Yoga teacher in Seattle says she had poor eating habits before she started practicing yoga 14 years ago. "I went for quick fixes for my energy needs, which meant lots of processed carbs and prepared foods," she says. "I ate too quickly. Burgers were common: lots of cheese, lots of bread."

Now she's much more aware of what and how she eats. She still has her comfort foods, but they're higher quality. "I love a grilled cheese sandwich, but these days I use good bread and cheese." Not only does Raffety choose healthful ingredients—her "good bread" is organic and whole grain—but she's also learned to deal with her emotions without turning to food, and she credits her meditation practice and yoga community with helping her do that. "A yoga community fosters healthy responses to difficult situations, whether it's mis-eating or anything else," she says.

While yoga and meditation can help you navigate the choppy waters of the American food industry, success won't happen overnight. But as you practice, you can build the discipline, patience, and compassion to overcome the many forces arrayed against you—no matter how formidable they seem.

The Forces Against You

We Americans, in our relentless pursuit of self-improvement, seem particularly vulnerable to the changing winds of nutritional expertise. As science writer Michael Pollan puts it, "We're a notably unhealthy people obsessed by the idea of eating healthily." It's a paradox the food industry and media regularly exploit. "Americans take a scientific view of food, not a pleasure view," says Pollan, the author of the [2006] *Omnivore's Dilemma: A Natural History of Four Meals.* "The food industry likes that because it frees them to reengineer processed foods to be low-fat or low-carb or high in omega-3s: whatever the wisdom *du jour* [of the day] calls for."

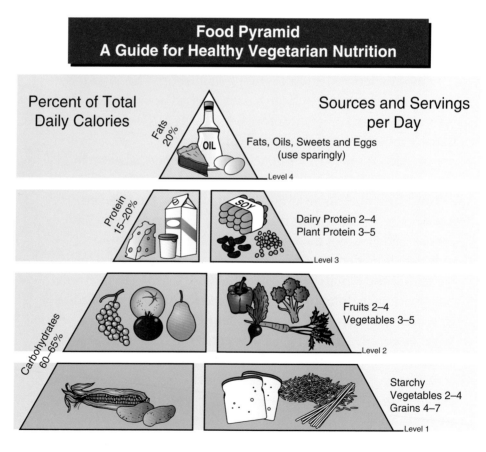

**Food Pyramid
A Guide for Healthy Vegetarian Nutrition**

Percent of Total
Daily Calories

Sources and Servings
per Day

Fats
20%

OIL

Fats, Oils, Sweets and Eggs
(use sparingly)
Level 4

Protein
15-20%

SOY

Dairy Protein 2–4
Plant Protein 3–5
Level 3

Carbohydrates
60–65%

Fruits 2–4
Vegetables 3–5
Level 2

Starchy
Vegetables 2–4
Grains 4–7
Level 1

Taken from: American Yoga Association

New York University nutrition professor Marion Nestle, who wrote *Food Politics*, believes that food manufacturers—just like companies that sell cigarettes, pharmaceuticals, or any other commodity—routinely place profit over public health. "Food companies," she says, "will make and market any product that sells, regardless of its nutritional value or its effect on health." And they want to sell as much of it as possible, which may be one reason government officials often hesitate to encourage Americans to eat less of any foods—even those like meat and full-fat dairy products, which are clearly harmful when eaten in large quantities.

"The government will never promote a message of 'Eat less,'" Pollan says. "It's trying to protect the public health while at the same time advance the mission of agriculture—an irreconcilable contradiction." Jane Hirschman, the coauthor of *Overcoming Overeating* and *When Women Stop Hating Their Bodies*, says, "The food industry would be half out of business if we ate only what our bodies required."

The Food Industry Markets Unhealthy Eating Habits

Instead, the food industry has tailored its products to be an antidote to emotional frustrations. Dietitian and diabetes educator Robin Edelman notes food marketers have capitalized on our innate sweet tooth by adding sugars to nearly every type of prepared food we buy—from vegetable soups to bottled waters—making it easy to consume up to 20 teaspoons a day.

And the more sugar we eat, the more we want. When we eat a piece of cake, for instance, the sweet taste triggers the brain to produce opioids, chemical messengers that identify the taste as desirable. At the same time, according to Elisabetta Politi, nutrition manager at the Duke University Diet & Fitness Center, the sweetness triggers the brain to produce dopamine, another chemical messenger that works with memory to urge us to pursue this rewarding taste in the future.

Moreover, Pollan claims that the food industry has "fractionated the marketplace by creating food designed for men, children, athletes, menopausal women, people eating in cars—you name it." . . . "The food industry's marketing machine is designed to subvert the family dinner," Pollan says.

An additional subverting influence is the fast-food industry. According to Pollan, research shows that 19 percent of American meals consist of food eaten in cars. Fully one in three children in America eats fast food daily. Despite all the research showing it to be nonnutritious, convenience and taste trump all.

As a final insult, the media—women's magazines, diet books, TV—conspire to make us feel insecure and unattractive, even as they purport to help us slim down. "We're regularly bombarded by images of perfect bodies," says Radhika Parameswaran, who teaches and does research on gender and media images at Indiana University. The result, she says, is that women are constantly comparing themselves to an impossible ideal.

That may explain why the U.S. weight-loss market was worth $46.3 billion last year [2005], according to Marketdata, a market research firm that tracks the weight-loss industry. But Americans remain chunkier than ever, with a 75 percent increase in adult obesity since 1991.

Clearly, we suffer from a dysfunctional attitude toward food. The ferocious marketing of every new diet makes us question every bite. Bananas, once considered nature's perfect food, are banned— along with all other fruit—from phase 1 of the South Beach Diet because its fructose spikes blood sugar levels. Bread, for centuries considered the staff of life, is now labeled too high in carbs. Fifteen years ago, a fat-free diet was the grail. More recently, dieters have been tucking into spreads of bacon, eggs, and beef. . . .

Yoga Leads to Mindful Eating

In the face of all this, how much help can yoga really offer? Plenty, as it turns out. Just ask Wade Wingler, a 34-year-old computer specialist in Indiana who has lost 100 pounds since starting yoga two years ago. "My success has been a series of small changes that have added up, but yoga is at the center of it," he says. "If I'm tempted to backslide in my eating, yoga helps me straighten up."

The belief that exercises such as yoga maintain healthy bodies better than diets alone is becoming more widespread.

His yoga practice, he says, has turned him into a much more mindful eater. Gone are the days of emotional or thoughtless eating; he's become attuned to his body's hunger signals. When he heeds them, he chooses food that's healthful and satisfying. And even though he still eats fast food, he's found ways to make it healthier and lower in calories. "I eat Wendy's chili or McDonald's side salad with grilled chicken. You have to ask them for this, but they'll do it."

Wingler has learned to moderate his intake and be less judgmental about food, which is key to changing eating habits, according to Michelle Stacey, the author of *Consumed: Why Americans Love, Hate, and Fear Food.* Her prescription for healthier eating is something she calls enlightened hedonism: eating satisfying food in smaller portions, without demonizing any food or food group. Her approach dispenses with the calculation of guilt, sacrifice, and indulgence so many of us fall prey to, silencing the voice that says, "I skipped breakfast, so I deserve this ice cream."

Other yogis say the practice has transformed their eating patterns completely. "I'm not attracted to lousy food anymore," says Anusara teacher Raffety. "Yoga has helped me realize how much junky food impairs my ability to think, to move." For Lynn Ginsburg, a 10-year yoga veteran and the author of *What Are You Hungry For?* the practice fine-tuned her palate and made her much pickier about her food. Junk food simply isn't appealing anymore.

With a more sensitive palate, you don't have to eat as much, especially since the gustatory pleasure of food is most intense in the first few bites. After that, diminishing returns set in. That's why three bites of dessert can often be completely satisfying. Of course, with the enormous portions served at restaurants, you may be tempted to eat everything on your plate. Until portion sizes are cut, however, you have to rely on your instincts to tell you when you are full.

Compassionate Eating

The kinder you are to yourself, the easier it will be, says Lisa Holtby, the author of *Healing Yoga for People Living with Cancer.* "Yoga calls us to practice compassion toward ourselves and others," she says, "so when I overeat, I've learned to say, 'What's up with the eating?' rather than beat myself up about it." Raffety credits that forgiving attitude for helping her change poor eating habits.

"Instead of pushing away bad foods, I move toward something that feels better, instead of making it about denial," she says.

Carré Otis, a model, TV producer, and yoga instructor in Marin County, California, who was anorexic for years, knows all too well the dangers of denial. "I was unsustainably thin," she says. Otis says her approach to food used to be based on how it would make her look, not on her health or well-being. "Yoga was a way for me to get into my body and learn to live in it," she says. "It was like finding my way back home." Her practice helped her see that size is irrelevant. As a result, she's comfortable relaxing the disciplined regimen of no processed foods that she once followed. "How can we expect the world to be full of lovingkindness when we can't even do it for ourselves?"

Lovingkindness is what Americans so desperately need. We won't be healthier about food until we learn to love it more, not less—with, as Stacey says, "a relaxed, unashamed emotion." And we may have to redefine the concept of "eating well." The phrase, says Stacey, is now "often used to convey the idea of a diet scientifically programmed to prevent disease, balanced to the last ounce with the nutrients the latest studies tout, and almost religiously outlawing certain forbidden foods."

Food as Comfort

But if you decide that no food is off limits, you can adopt a more relaxed and social approach toward eating. You're likely to find yourself enjoying the journey instead of focusing on the destination, just as yoga teaches, says Timothy McCall, the author of the [2007] *Yoga as Medicine*. "Rather than saying, 'I'm going to lose 20 pounds by spring,' say, 'I'm going to become more mindful of my eating.'"

As you do this, the joys of eating will reveal themselves. Sharon Gannon, the co-owner and codirector of Jivamukti Yoga Centers in New York City, finds eating a magical experience. "You take one substance into your body that then becomes your body," she says. Gannon tries to imbue her food "with my intention to bring more happiness into the world." . . .

This search for answers may mask a deeper longing for a sense of purpose. We've become so engrossed in dodging illness that we've forgotten, as [chef and author Jacques] Pepin says, "that the point of living is to enjoy."

Your practice can help restore that focus. It can remind you to fixate less on your diet and more on fulfilling your potential to be creatively engaged with the world, working in service to some cause greater than yourself.

NINE

Dieting Does Not Work

Stuart Wolpert

In the following article, Stuart Wolpert presents research conducted by the University of California, Los Angeles, that shows diets do not work. According to Wolpert, the study shows that while people may lose up to 10 percent of their weight on various diets, most people gain back all of the weight they lost; and often they end up weighing more than before going on the diet. One of the psychologists Wolpert interviews states that most people would have been better off never dieting in the first place. Stuart Wolpert is an author for *UCLA News*.

Will you lose weight and keep it off if you diet? No, probably not, UCLA [University of California, Los Angeles] researchers report in the April [2007] issue of *American Psychologist*, the journal of the American Psychological Association.

"You can initially lose 5 to 10 percent of your weight on any number of diets, but then the weight comes back," said Traci Mann, UCLA associate professor of psychology and lead author of the study. "We found that the majority of people regained all the weight, plus more. Sustained weight loss was found only in a small minority of participants, while complete weight regain was

Stuart Wolpert, "Dieting Does Not Work, UCLA Researchers Report," *UCLA News*, April 3, 2007. Reproduced by permission

Many scientists believe fitness may play a bigger role than dieting, regardless of the type of exercise.

found in the majority. Diets do not lead to sustained weight loss or health benefits for the majority of people."

Mann and her co-authors conducted the most comprehensive and rigorous analysis of diet studies, analyzing 31 long-term studies.

"What happens to people on diets in the long run?" Mann asked. "Would they have been better off to not go on a diet at all? We decided to dig up and analyze every study that followed people on diets for two to five years. We concluded most of them would have been better off not going on the diet at all. Their weight would be pretty much the same, and their bodies would not suffer the wear and tear from losing weight and gaining it all back."

People on diets typically lose 5 to 10 percent of their starting weight in the first six months, the researchers found. However, at least one-third to two-thirds of people on diets regain more weight than they lost within four or five years, and the true number may well be significantly higher, they said.

"Although the findings reported give a bleak picture of the effectiveness of diets, there are reasons why the actual effectiveness of diets is even worse," Mann said.

Past Diets Predict Future Weight Gain

Mann said that certain factors biased the diet studies to make them appear more effective than they really were. For one, many participants self-reported their weight by phone or mail rather than having their weight measured on a scale by an impartial source. Also, the studies have very low follow-up rates—eight of the studies had follow-up rates lower than 50 percent, and those who responded may not have been representative of the entire group, since people who gain back large amounts of weight are generally unlikely to show up for follow-up tests, Mann said.

"Several studies indicate that dieting is actually a consistent predictor of future weight gain," said Janet Tomiyama, a UCLA graduate student of psychology and co-author of the study. One study found that both men and women who participated in formal weight-loss programs gained significantly more weight over a two-year period than those who had not participated in a weight-loss program, she said.

Another study, which examined a variety of lifestyle factors and their relationship to changes in weight in more than 19,000 healthy older men over a four-year period, found that "one of the best predictors of weight gain over the four years was having lost weight on a diet at some point during the years before the study started," Tomiyama said. In several studies, people in control groups who did not diet were not that much worse off—and in many cases were better off—than those who did diet, she said.

If Dieting Doesn't Work, What Does?

"Eating in moderation is a good idea for everybody, and so is regular exercise," Mann said. "That is not what we looked at in this study. Exercise may well, be the key factor leading to sustained weight loss. Studies consistently find that people who reported the most exercise also had the most weight loss."

Diet studies of less than two years are too short to show whether dieters have regained the weight they lost, Mann said.

"Even when you follow dieters four years, they're still regaining weight," she said.

One study of dieting obese patients followed them for varying lengths of time. Among those who were followed for fewer than two years, 23 percent gained back more weight than they had lost, while of those who were followed for at least two years, 83 percent gained back more weight than they had lost, Mann said. One study found that 50 percent of dieters weighed more than 11 pounds over their starting weight five years after the diet, she said.

Evidence suggests that repeatedly losing and gaining weight is linked to cardiovascular disease, stroke, diabetes and altered immune function. Mann and Tomiyama recommend that more research be conducted on the health effects of losing and gaining weight, noting that scientists do not fully understand how such weight cycling leads to adverse health effects.

Mann notes that her mother has tried different diets, and has not succeeded in keeping the weight off. "My mother has been on diets and says what we are saying is obvious," she said.

While the researchers analyzed 31 dieting studies, they have not evaluated specific diets.

Dieting Does Not Treat Obesity

Medicare raised the issue of whether obesity is an illness, deleting the words "Obesity is not considered an illness" from its coverage regulations in 2004. The move may open the door for Medicare to consider funding treatments for obesity, Mann noted.

"Diets are not effective in treating obesity," said Mann. "We are recommending that Medicare should not fund weight-loss programs as a treatment for obesity. The benefits of dieting are too small and the potential harm is too large for dieting to be recommended as a safe, effective treatment for obesity."

Ten Ideas to Get Active

Adults

1. Use a push mower to mow the lawn.
2. Go for a walk in a nearby park.
3. Take the stairs instead of an elevator.
4. Bike to work, to run errands, or visit friends.
5. Clean out the garage or the attic.
6. Walk with a friend over the lunch hour.
7. Volunteer to become a coach or referee.
8. Sign up for a group exercise class.
9. Join a softball league.
10. Park at the farthest end of the lot.

Kids

1. Take your dog out for a walk.
2. Start up a playground kickball game.
3. Join a sports team.
4. Go to the park with a friend.
5. Help your parents with yardwork.
6. Play tag with kids in your neighborhood.
7. Ride your bike to school.
8. Walk to the store for your mom.
9. See how many jumping jacks you can do.
10. Race a friend to the end of the block.

Taken from: www.presidentschallenge.org

From 1980 to 2000, the percentage of Americans who were obese more than doubled, from 15 percent to 31 percent of the population, Mann noted.

A social psychologist, Mann, taught a UCLA graduate seminar on the psychology of eating four years ago. She and her students continued the research when the course ended. Mann's co-authors are Erika Westling, Ann-Marie Lew, Barbra Samuels and Jason Chatman.

"We asked what evidence is there that dieting works in the long term, and found that the evidence shows the opposite" Tomiyama said.

The research was partially supported by the National Institute of Mental Health.

In future research, Mann is interested in studying whether a combination of diet and exercise is more effective than exercise alone.

Calorie Restriction
Is an Extreme
Way to Diet

Julian Dibbell

> In the following article, Julian Dibbell reports on his expe-
> rience practicing the extreme Calorie Restriction (CR)
> diet. He explains that CR is a cultish diet in which the
> participants live on the edge of starvation. Dibbell uses a
> dinner party thrown for a group of veteran CR followers to
> set the stage for his experience. Dibbell writes that he had
> been living on 1,800 calories per day—700 calories less
> than the recommended number for adult males. Dibbell
> reveals that the ultimate goal of Calorie Restriction dieters
> is to dramatically improve their health and well-being and
> to increase their life span. Julian Dibbell is an author and
> contributing editor for *Wired* magazine.

I've been starving for the past two months, actually, and that's
precisely what the party is about: My dinner guests—five successful urban professionals who for years have subsisted on a caloric
intake the average sub-Saharan African would find austere—have
been at it much, much longer, and I've invited them here to
show me how it's done. They are master practitioners of Calorie
Restriction [CR], a diet whose central, radical premise is that the
less you eat, the longer you'll live. Having taken this diet for a
nine-week test drive, I'm hoping now for an up-close glimpse of

what it means to go all the way. I want to find out what it looks, feels, and tastes like to commit to the ultimate in dietary trade-offs: a lifetime lived as close to the brink of starvation as your body can stand, in exchange for the promise of a life span longer than any human has ever known.

Seat belts, vaccines, clean tap water, and other modern miracles have dramatically boosted average life expectancies, to be sure—reducing annually the percentage of people who die before reaching the maximum life span—but CR alone demonstrably raises the maximum itself. In lab studies going back to the thirties, mice on severely limited diets have consistently lived as much as 50 percent longer than the oldest of their well-fed peers—the rodent equivalent of a human life stretched past the age of 160. And it isn't just a mouse thing: Yeast cells, spiders, vinegar worms, rhesus monkey—by now a veritable menagerie of species has been shown to benefit from CR's life-extending effects.

Despite the mounting evidence, however, the link between CR and longevity remained for many years a medical curiosity, its implications for human health intriguing, certainly, but unexplored. Partly this was because nobody, to this day, has figured out exactly how the CR effect works. Some have suggested that the threat of starvation triggers certain self-preservative responses in animal physiologies; others have pursued a sort of "fuel efficiency" hypothesis, proposing that lightening the body's load of food-energy processing reduces wear and tear on cellular machinery. But no one theory has ever settled the question firmly enough to prove that humans would benefit from CR as much as other animals have. That has left direct experimentation as the next best route to an answer, and for obvious reasons, finding human subjects willing to live on concentration-camp diets has historically been a tricky proposition.

Biosphere 2
In 1991, however, the proposition was simplified somewhat when a team of eight bioscientists sealed themselves up for a two-year stint inside a giant, airtight terrarium in the Arizona desert—

and promptly discovered that the hypothetically self-sustaining ecosystem they'd settled into could barely grow enough food to keep them alive. This revelation might have doomed the experiment (known as Biosphere 2) but for the fact that the team's physician, UCLA pathologist Roy Walford, had been studying the Calorie Restriction phenomenon for decades and convinced his fellow econauts that—as long as they all ate carefully enough

A participant in a calorie-restriction study shows that rapid weight loss can occur when severely restricting calories in a diet program.

to get their daily share of essential nutrients—a year or two of near starvation wouldn't hurt. When at last the Biosphere 2 crew emerged from their bubble, tests proved them healthier in nearly every nutritionally relevant respect than when they'd gone in, and the case for Calorie Restriction in humans was no longer purely circumstantial. Fifteen years later, Walford's CR primer, *Beyond the 120-Year Diet: How to Double Your Vital Years*, is in its fifth printing, and an estimated 1,400 people have taken up the diet as a full-time, lifelong practice.

It isn't hard to see the diet's appeal to a certain very familiar New York type: You're skinnier than any social X-ray, you're practicing a regimen as extreme and as grueling as any yogi's, and you've got some impressive medical science on your side. For someone attracted to control, accomplishment, and power, this is the life. And I'm living it.

The hardest part, I find, is the math: not just the labor of tracking everything I put in my body but the way in which calorie counting makes the no-free-lunch adage so viscerally clear. Bacon cheeseburgers, chocolate, a martini—all are pleasures now completely ruined by the knowledge that the massive caloric debts that they create must be paid for with days or even weeks of caloric cutbacks. Other abnegations—the dinner invitations regretfully declined, the awkward orders of soda water on the rocks at "drinks" with friends and colleagues, the freakishly ascetic feeling of sitting gaunt and empty-plated before a calorie-packed family dinner— are met with the compensatory feeling one gets when walking a righteous, if lonely, path. . . .

Below Normal BMI

The 1,800 daily calories I've been consuming fall well short of the minimum 2,500 recommended for adult males, and two months on this caloric budget has shrunk my 43-year-old, five-eleven frame from an almost officially overweight 178 pounds to a high-school-era 157. Friends and loved ones, I've noticed, have started sounding more concerned than impressed when they see how much weight I've lost, but here within the charmed circle of tonight's dinner party, I don't feel so much scrawny as trim—dashing, even. Standing around the kitchen's broad butcher-block prep table with these five world-class calorie restricters, I recognize our thinness as sophisticated and sane, the height of a slender, Nick and Nora Charles [characters in the 1934 film; *The Thin Man*] sort of elegance.

Though I'm our official host, it's the compact, wisecracking April Smith who presides. April has volunteered to plan and cook tonight's CR-correct menu, and her sous-chef for the evening, Michael, stands beside her at the ready: a boyish-looking 35-year-old with brush-cut red hair, translucently pale skin, and—at six feet tall and 115 pounds—an eerily spare physique.

Consider those dimensions for a moment. Divide Michael's weight by the square of his height and you get a body-mass index [BMI] of 15.6. Compare that with the minimum BMI of 18 recently decreed by the organizers of the Madrid Fashion Week—who cited the World Health Organization's definition of 18.5 as the lower limit of healthy weight and offered medical assistance to any models who couldn't meet it—and you might wonder how Michael can stand up in the morning, let alone jog twenty miles a week. But jog he does, and if the results of both his latest physical and the latest CR research are anything to go by, Michael is probably one of the healthiest 35-year-olds on the planet. . . .

Awake, Energetic, and Euphoric

It's no secret. From mystics to anorexics, people who go for long periods without eating often report feeling more awake and energetic, even euphoric. It's nice for a while, but even the calorie-restricted can get too much of it. When April started CR, she often went long stretches between meals and eventually decided something was a little off. "It makes you feel like you're on drugs; I got too euphoric," she says. "You know, thinking you're in love when you're not." She switched to a more consistent, balanced eating schedule, came back down to Earth, and that, she says with a shrug, was that:

"It's like, 'Eat something! You're *not* in love.'"

Weighing Your Risk

Body Mass Index (BMI)		Waist less than or equal to 40 in. (men) or 35 in. (women)	Waist greater than 40 in. (men) or 35 in. (women)
18.5 or less	Underweight	–	N/A
18.6 - 24.9	Normal	–	N/A
25.0 - 29.9	Overweight	Increased	High
30.0 - 34.9	Obese	High	Very High
35.0 - 39.9	Obese	Very High	Very High
40 or greater	Extremely Obese	Extremely High	Extremely High

Taken from: www.pueblo.gsa.gov

April brings the main course: a medley of asparagus tips, shiitake mushrooms, and the featured ingredient, an unlikely hybrid of life-giving wholesomeness and bio-industrial hubris known as Quorn.

Quorn, at last! For as long as I've been following the blogs and mailing lists of the greater Calorie Restriction community, I've been reading about this patented wonder morsel, perhaps the ultimate in CR-friendly foods. Grown in fermentation tanks from a cultured strain of the soil mold *Fusarium venenatum*, Quorn in its virgin state is almost pure protein and very low in calories. Processing adds various essential nutrients, including a generous helping of zinc, which is concentrated in almost no other food but oysters and which the calorie-restricted can never get enough of. The end product tastes and chews remarkably like an unbreaded Chicken McNugget and can substitute for meat with all the versatility of soy (Quorn dogs, Quorn cutlets, and Quorn roasts are just a few of the *faux*-flesh varieties on offer) yet with fewer saturated fats and none of the alleged dementia-and/or-male-aggression-causing properties. . . .

For dessert, we get a CR-perfect parfait: organic strawberries, nonfat ricotta, flaxseed oil, and hazelnuts. It's very good, and it's gone too fast, and as long as we're rewriting the book on table manners here, I can't see the harm in scooping out the last bits of ricotta with my fingers. April sees me and frowns, concerned. "You need to eat more. Like right now," she says, bringing me seconds.

This of course is just the sort of swift correction any responsible CR veteran would apply to a fellow calorie restricter showing signs of manorexia. But with April, there's a little more to it than that. She's a woman, for one thing, which the typical CR veteran is not, and that alone makes her more than typically familiar with the feminine cult of self-starvation and its costs. Beyond that, too, she brings a special knowledge with her from her high-school years, spent at the Interlochen Arts Academy—a peculiarly intense Midwestern boarding school lately prominent in the literature of eating disorders, having served as the central setting for the acclaimed memoir of anorexia and bulimia *Wasted*, by April's Interlochen classmate Marya Hornbacher.

"I have a ton of survivor's guilt for being one of the ones who made it out alive, you know? Because so many of my close friends have been down that path," says April. "When we were in high school, everybody was doing it. Interlochen was a performing-arts school where dancers were graded down for gaining weight. And we all used to think we were fat and be miserable about our bodies. And, you know, when I started CR, there were questions like, 'Oh, have you gone anorexic?'"

"But they are such complete opposites," April insists. "The focus of CR is health. Nobody here is trying to figure out how to eat less and disappear. The constant thought is, 'How can I pack more nutrition into my calories?—and that's not something an anorexic is doing. Anorexia is slow suicide.'" . . .

Late in the morning on the first day after my dinner party, I awaken hungry, go downstairs, walk into the first McDonald's I encounter, and consume, for breakfast, an entire Quarter Pounder with cheese and a 12-ounce chocolate triple-thick shake. Later, at the cocktail hour, I drink several Cuba Libres and eat cheese-laden canapés to my heart's content. For dinner, I stop in at Katz's Delicatessen on Houston Street and ingest one half of a two-inch-thick pastrami on rye, half a corned-beef sandwich just as massive, several pickled tomatoes, and a cream soda, and only after eating a slab of chocolate-coated Häagen-Dazs ice cream on a stick at bedtime do I begin to feel the first, light pangs of queasiness. For the first time in 63 days, I end the day without the slightest idea how many calories I ate or the least desire to know.

You would think it would have taken more than a few unkind remarks about Quorn to cancel my date with a calorie-restricted destiny, and you would be right, of course. Adam's [author's friend who also attended the dinner party] skepticism got me thinking, is all—not so much about how the food tasted to him as about how the whole evening must have looked to him, and for that matter, how it might have looked to me just a few months earlier. The slightly messianic tint to Paul McGlothin's every utterance; the casual yet total confidence with which Don and Michael had discussed their prospects for eternal life on Earth, like two born-again Christians guessing at the precise date of the Rapture. I liked these people, I really did. But in the end, I made my way home that night with the growing sense that I had just come closer than I ever had to falling down the bottomless black hole of cult membership.

ELEVEN

Teenagers Should Not Diet

Kelly Burgess

Kelly Burgess discusses the eating habits of teenagers with two nutritionists. Burgess tries to get to the bottom of the question, "should teenagers diet?" The author finds that the answer is "no." The nutritionists Burgess interviewed agreed that teenagers could use an overhaul on what they eat—refined sugars and junk food—but stated that it is dangerous for teens to go on fad diets, such as Atkins, because such diets deplete calcium, a very important nutrient for growing bones. The author also discovered that teens who diet are at higher risk for developing eating disorders, and girls, in particular risk losing bone mass. Kelly Burgess is a senior writer for *iParenting Media*.

I was floored when my 16-year-old daughter told me that her best friend's soccer coach had put the entire girls' soccer team on a low-carbohydrate diet. After all, in the reams of writing I've done on the subject of childhood nutrition, there are a few general "rules" about kids and food that seem to come up over and over. They are:

1. Teenagers should never diet.

Burgess, Kelly, "Low-Carb Diets and Teens: Nonsense or Common Sense?" *iParenting,* 2007. www .teenagerstoday.com/redirect.php?page=/resources/articles/lowcarbteens.htmAppendix

2. Girls should never be told they need to diet.
3. Girls who diet risk loss of bone mass.
4. Female athletes who diet risk loss of bone mass, cessation of menses and eating disorders.
5. Low-carbohydrate diets are bad for everyone.

So my question became this: How do these "rules" apply to low-carb diets and teens? What I discovered is that while numbers 1 through 4 are absolutely true, 5 is definitely open to a healthy interpretation.

Teens and Dieting

Katie Bark, nutritionist and special project coordinator for the Team Nutrition Program at the Montana State University Department of Health and Human Development, says that rule No. 1 is unequivocally true.

"Teens should not be on a diet, because we don't want to teach young people to diet, and we don't want them to develop that diet mentality," says Bark.

She's right to be concerned. According to the American Academy of Child and Adolescent Psychiatry (AACAP), eating disorders are on the increase among teenage girls and young women. AACAP estimates that as many as 10 in 100 young women suffer from the two most serious eating disorders, anorexia nervosa and bulimia. This disordered eating comes from a variety of societal factors, and encouraging teens to "diet" is no solution. Rather, says Bark, the family should focus on good eating and exercise habits all the time.

And there's the rub. Because the fact is, teens don't generally have good exercise habits, nor do they have a well-rounded diet. Unfortunately, teens, even relatively amenable, well-informed teens like Bark's two teenage daughters and my teenagers, like to eat junk. Soda pop, burgers, French fries and potato chips are much more attractive to teens than grilled fish and steamed veggies—no matter how lovingly the healthy dish is prepared.

Low Carb = Low Sugar

When I told nutritionist Carol Simontacchi the soccer team story, her answer was, "Good. At least they're cutting back on their sugar!"

She went on to qualify her initial reaction with an assurance that she does not like fad diets, does not like the idea of teens being on diets and thinks that Atkins is not a healthful low-carb approach. However, she also said the fact is that kids eat too much processed foods, eat and drink too much sugar and too many chemicals, and, in general, a low-carb diet can't be much worse than what they're already putting into their bodies.

Simontacchi should know. She's the author of *The Crazy Makers: How the Food Industry Is Destroying Our Brains and Harming Our Children* and the mother of four children who don't always appreciate her nutritional expertise.

"The reality is that kids' eating habits are so bad at this point that if a low-carb diet can get them off junk food and soft drinks, it will be doing some good," says Simontacchi. "Yes, some of the diets encourage a lot of red meat, but which is more harmful, red meat or 46 ounces of soft drinks?"

What low-carb diets do encourage that Simontacchi thinks is a good trend is vegetables. "Maybe low-carb is not good, but they're now eating three servings of vegetables a day, up from zero servings before," says Simontacchi. "Maybe it will balance their blood sugar, and that's simply not a bad thing."

Bad Carbs, Good Carbs

Nori Hudson is another fan of low-carb diets—within reason. Hudson, a nutritionist and educator, says the problem with almost everyone's diet is that we eat like marathon runners and then sit on the couch.

"Carbs are the body's preferred source of energy, but when we don't use those carbs, the body turns it to fat," says Hudson. "The foods that tend to be quick foods are usually over-processed carbohydrates, such as potato chips and crackers. These are not foods anyone should be eating."

Like Bark and Simontacchi, Hudson notes that no young person should diet. However, she deplores the eating habits of today's teens and, like Simontacchi, thinks a low-carb diet can lead to some improvement in eating habits—if it's done in a healthful manner.

In other words, low-carb isn't necessarily unhealthy, just the recent fad diets that promote it, such as Atkins. "The Atkins diet is simply too restrictive to be healthful for a teen who is growing and putting down 50 percent of their calcium in the bone bank for future bone health." says Bark.

A recent study published in the *National Library of Medicine* justifies Bark's concerns. It showed strong anecdotal evidence that a low-carb diet followed for as little as six weeks can increase the risk for bone loss. While this is not desirable at any age group, it can be particularly devastating to the long-term bone health of teenage girls who are following Atkins-type diets, which severely limit healthy calcium sources.

However, a diet that restricts processed carbohydrates, such as white breads, potato chips and sugary snacks, in favor of high-quality carbohydrates such as fruit, vegetables and whole grains, is an excellent choice for anyone. Pair that with protein sources that are lower in saturated fats, such as poultry and fish, and low-fat dairy products, such as skim milk and fat-free yogurts, and you have a healthy diet.

Is it low-carb? It is if you compare it to what teens normally eat. Is it healthy? Absolutely, as long as the idea is to make healthful food choices and not to restrict calories.

Those Wild Teen Eaters

And now back to my daughter's best friend's diet. She wasn't on it for three minutes before she was eating pizza in my kitchen. Why? Because she's a teenager, that's why.

There's so much research showing that teens are hardwired to do the opposite of whatever it is their parents want them to do that quoting it here would make this article a book. So I'll just quote my experts, Bark and Simontacchi, two nutritionists with six teenagers between them.

"My kids have been brought up on a healthy diet and been taught extensively about good nutrition, but they're teens and they're eating stuff they know I don't like, and I hate it," says Simontacchi. "One day, I said to my daughter, 'I'm a nutritionist and this is what my kids are bringing into my house?' Her answer was that if I saw what the other kids are eating, I would see that I had really made progress with them."

"I have two daughters, 17 and 16, and it's so normal for them to exert their independence by going out to eat," says Bark. "It can make you crazy, but you really have to be careful not to push, or they go even further in the other direction."

Both professional and personal experiences have taught Bark and Simontacchi that keeping the lines of communication open is important. If your child tells you she is on or wants to be on a low-carb diet, make sure she understands what healthy choices she can make within those parameters. Explain the pros and cons of low-carb—particularly the concerns about loss of bone mass—and make sure he or she has healthy, low-carb choices at home, since those that are offered in restaurants and fast-food places often rely heavily on unhealthy, saturated fats.

Simontacchi says that making deals works also. For example, tell him that you'll support his low-carb diet approach if he promises to eat at least two vegetables per day.

And don't give up. Like many other things that they do from the time they're toddlers until they hit about 30, this, too, shall pass. Eventually, they will grow out of the teen junk food phase and remember the good food habits you've always tried to instill.

What You Should Know About Dieting

Facts About Men and Weight
- Men's body image is less negative than women's.
- Underweight men experience more emotional problems than overweight men.
- Anorexia and bulimia are still fairly uncommon in men, but young men are most prone.
- Men are most likely to use anabolic steroids in their quest for greater muscle mass.
- One million boys and men struggle with eating disorders and borderline conditions.
- On any given day, one in four men are on a diet.
- 68.3 million men (70.5 percent) are overweight.
- 28.6 million men (29.5 percent) are obese.
- 27.4 million men (28.3 percent) are at a healthy weight.

Facts About Women and Weight
- The average American woman is five feet, four inches tall, weighs 140 pounds, and wears a size fourteen dress.
- One-third of all American women wear a size sixteen or larger.
- Seventy-five percent of American women are dissatisfied with their appearance.
- Fifty percent of American women are on a diet at any one time.
- Young girls are more afraid of becoming fat than they are of nuclear war, cancer, or losing their parents.

- Fifty percent of nine-year-old girls and 80 percent of ten-year-old girls have dieted.
- Ninety percent of high school junior and senior women diet regularly, even though only between 10 percent and 15 percent are over the weight recommended by the standard height-weight charts.
- One percent of teenage girls and 5 percent of college-age women become anorexic or bulimic.
- Anorexia has the highest mortality rate (up to 20 percent) of any psychiatric diagnosis.
- Young girls develop eating and self-image problems before drug or alcohol problems.
- Women in one study reported being afraid to eat dairy products, because they worried dairy would make them gain weight. This means that they are starving themselves into osteoporosis.

Facts About Dieting
- Between 90 percent and 99 percent of reducing diets fail to produce permanent weight loss.
- Two-thirds of dieters regain the weight they lost within one year.
- Virtually all dieters regain their initial weight within five years.
- The diet industry earns over $40 billion each year.
- Quick weight-loss schemes are among the most common consumer frauds.
- Diet programs have the highest customer dissatisfaction of any service industry.
- A recent survey found only 30 percent of 250 randomly chosen women age twenty-one to thirty-five had normal bone mass.
- Growing teens should consume at least eighteen hundred calories per day; most diets recommend fewer calories.
- Eating too few calories can cause muscle proteins to break down, causing muscle death—some diets can cause a 3 to 6 percent loss of muscle density.

- When a person does not consume enough carbohydrates, the body goes into "starvation mode."
- High-protein, low-carb diets can raise cholesterol to dangerously high levels.
- Yo-yo dieting leads to decreased metabolism.

Facts About Obesity

- Approximately 1.6 billion adults (over age fifteen) were overweight in 2005.
- At least 400 million adults were obese in 2005.
- The World Health Organization projects that by 2015, approximately 2.3 billion adults will be overweight and more than 700 million will be obese.
- At least 20 million children in the world under the age of five were overweight in 2005.
- Once considered a problem only in high-income countries, obesity is now dramatically on the rise in low- and middle-income countries, particularly in urban settings.

Consequences of Being Overweight or Obese

- Cardiovascular disease (mainly heart disease and stroke) kills 17 million people each year.
- The incidence of heart disease (heart attack, congestive heart failure, sudden cardiac death, angina or chest pain, and abnormal heart rhythm) is increased in persons who are overweight or obese (BMI > 25).
- High blood pressure is twice as common in adults who are obese than in those who are at a healthy weight.
- Obesity is associated with elevated triglycerides (blood fat) and decreased HDL (good cholesterol).
- A weight gain of eleven to eighteen pounds increases a person's risk of developing type 2 diabetes to twice that of individuals who have not gained weight.
- Musculoskeletal disorders—especially osteoarthritis—occur more often in adults who are obese.

- Some cancers (endometrial, breast, and colon) occur more often in adults who are obese.
- Women gaining more than twenty pounds from age eighteen to midlife double their risk of postmenopausal breast cancer, compared to women whose weight remains stable.
- An estimated three hundred thousand deaths per year may be attributable to obesity.
- Individuals who are obese (BMI > 30) have a 50 to 100 percent increased risk of premature death from all causes, compared to individuals with a healthy weight.
- Sleep apnea (interrupted breathing while sleeping) is more common in obese persons.
- Obesity is associated with a higher prevalence of asthma.
- For every two-pound increase in weight, the risk of developing arthritis is increased by 9 to 13 percent.
- Overweight and obesity are associated with increased risk of gall bladder disease, incontinence, increased surgical risk, and depression.
- Obesity during pregnancy is associated with increased risk of death in both the baby and the mother and increases the risk of maternal high blood pressure by ten times.
- Obesity during pregnancy is associated with an increased risk of birth defects, particularly neural tube defects, such as spina bifida.
- Infants born to women who are obese during pregnancy are more likely to have a high birth weight and, therefore, may face a higher rate of Cesarean section delivery and low blood sugar (which can be associated with brain damage and seizures).
- Obesity can affect the quality of life through limited mobility and decreased physical endurance as well as through social, academic, and job discrimination.
- The cost of obesity in the United States in 2000 was more than $117 billion ($61 billion direct and $56 billion indirect).

What You Should Do About Dieting

Educate Yourself

The first step on the road to weight loss is to become educated about your body. Start out by finding the answers to these questions: Look into your family's history—is obesity in your genes? Why do you want to lose weight? How much do you weigh? What is your BMI (body mass index)? What diet plan will work best for you?

People who come from a family that tends toward obesity will find that their fight to lose excess pounds will be more difficult than those who do not. A child with obese parents is more than twice as likely to become an obese adult as a child whose parents are not obese. Parents of overweight kids should model healthy eating habits, and families should eat together when possible. Establishing good eating habits at an early age can help combat fat genes.

If you decide to go on a diet, be sure to thoroughly research the method you select. Your choice should depend on how much weight you need to lose. This should be a joint decision between you, your family, and your doctor.

Assess Your Diet and Weight

Before you go on a diet, make sure you *need* to lose weight. Talk with your parent about seeing a doctor or nutritionist to discuss your age, body type, weight, exercise level, and mental health. These professionals will determine if you must lose weight and will recommend how many pounds you should lose. They will also help you to see that there is more to weight loss than just dropping pounds, and that choosing a diet that is wrong for you can have dangerous, even lethal consequences. There are many ways to lose weight—but it is very important to do so safely no matter which weight-loss method you choose to follow.

Evaluate your diet. Keep a journal of everything you consume (meals, drinks, snacks, etc.) for three days. Pay special attention to the times of day that you tend to binge or snack on empty calories. Notice where you are lacking in nutrition and get ready to research how you can change your diet to live a more healthful lifestyle. When you evaluate your weight and are ready to make the decision whether to go on a diet, be sure to consider the following:

• Your height
• Your body type
• Your genetics
• Your overall health and well-being

Body mass index (BMI) measures body fat based on your height and weight and is one way that your physician may evaluate your weight. BMI falls into the following categories:

• Underweight: BMI < 18.5
• Normal weight: BMI = 18.5–24.9
• Overweight: BMI = 25–29.9
• Obesity: BMI > 30 or greater

The body mass index does have limitations. It may overestimate the body fat in athletes who have high muscle mass. It may also underestimate body fat in the elderly who have lost muscle mass with aging.

Your weight is just a number, but looking at all of the above issues will give you a full picture and help indicate what your weight means and what it should be. What you think you should weigh and what you should actually weigh are often dramatically different numbers when you look at the whole picture.

Create an Action Plan
If you know that you must lose weight, it's a good idea to create a plan of action. Use the food journal that you created to isolate

problem areas with your diet. Plan to incorporate an exercise regimen into your daily routine. Sit down and write out your goals. Make sure they are realistic. Break down larger goals such as, "I want to lose a hundred pounds," to "I will lose one to two pounds per week." Making goals that you can easily attain will help keep you motivated and safe.

Remember, motivation to lose weight can make or break any diet. If you are trying to lose weight for someone else (a boyfriend or girlfriend, parent, etc.), the odds of sticking to your diet are slim. However, if you have made the decision for yourself based on your health and well-being, then you will be much more successful.

The following steps can safely be followed by everyone and can lead to the National Institutes of Health recommendation to lose no more than one to three pounds per month, depending on your starting weight.

- Set realistic short-term goals that are flexible.
- Eat breakfast every day.
- Reward successes.
- Keep a daily food log.
- Do thirty minutes of some kind of physical activity every day.
- Reduce portions.
- Eat less, more often.
- Avoid activities that cause you to overeat (such as excessive TV watching).
- Be kind to yourself when you look in the mirror.

The key to any successful weight-loss program is support. Involve your friends and family in your efforts, and remember that your ultimate goal should be to get healthy, not skinny. Once you decide to make healthy choices, you will see that you have more energy and that you will want to continue to eat well and exercise, because the rewards materialize fairly quickly. Remember that success breeds more success!

American Academy of Child and Adolescent Psychiatry (AACAP)
3615 Wisconsin Avenue NW, Washington, DC 20016
(202) 966-7300
fax: (202) 966-2891
Web site: www.aacap.org

AACAP is a nonprofit organization dedicated to providing parents and families with information regarding developmental, behavioral, and mental disorders that affect children and adolescents. The organization provides national public information through the distribution of the newsletter *Facts for Families* and the monthly *Journal of the American Academy of Child and Adolescent Psychiatry.*

American Dietetic Association (ADA)
216 West Jackson Boulevard, Suite 800, Chicago, IL 60606
(312) 899-0040
fax: (312) 899-1979
Web site: www.eatright.org

ADA is the largest organization of food and nutrition professionals in the United States. It works to shape the food choices and nutritional status of the public for optimal nutrition, health, and well-being. The association publishes the monthly *Journal of the American Dietetic Association* as well as a variety of booklets, pamphlets, and fact sheets about nutrition.

American Heart Association (AHA)
7272 Greenville Avenue, Dallas, TX 75231
Web site: www.americanheart.org

The AHA is committed to fighting heart disease and stroke and to raising awareness of these diseases. As part of their mission, they focus on specific causes designed to help people achieve a heart-healthy lifestyle. Each of their cause initiatives reaches out to the public with resources and information to help people take positive action.

American Society for Bariatric Surgery
100 SW 75th Street, Suite 201, Gainesville, FL 32607
Web site: www.asbs.org

The purpose of the American Society for Bariatric Surgery is to advance the art and science of bariatric surgery by encouraging its members to pursue investigations in both the clinic and the laboratory; to exchange ideas, information, and experience pertaining to bariatric surgery; to promote guidelines for ethical patient selection and care; to develop educational programs for physicians, paramedical persons, and lay people; and to promote outcome studies and quality assurance.

Anorexia Nervosa and Related Eating Disorders (ANRED)
PO Box 5102, Eugene, OR 97405
(503) 344-1144
Web site: www.anred.com

ANRED is a nonprofit organization that provides information about anorexia nervosa, bulimia nervosa, binge eating disorder, compulsive exercising, and other lesser-known food and weight disorders, including details about recovery and prevention. ANRED offers workshops, individual and professional training, and local community education. It also produces a monthly newsletter.

Centers for Disease Control and Prevention (CDC)
1600 Clifton Road, NE, Atlanta, GA 30333
(404) 639-3311or (404) 639-3534
Web site: www.cdc.gov

The CDC strives to protect people's health and safety, to provide reliable health information, and to improve health through strong partnerships. The steps needed to accomplish this mission are based on scientific excellence, requiring well-trained public health practitioners and leaders dedicated to high standards of quality and ethical practice.

Eating Disorders Awareness and Prevention. (EDAP)
603 Stewart Street, Suite 803, Seattle, WA 98101
(206) 382-3587
fax: (206) 292-9890
Web site: http://members.aol.com/edapinc

EDAP is dedicated to promoting the awareness and prevention of eating disorders by encouraging positive self-esteem and size acceptance. It provides free and low-cost educational information on eating disorders and how to prevent them. EDAP also provides educational outreach programs and training for schools and universities and sponsors the Puppet Project for Schools and the annual National Eating Disorders Awareness Week. EDAP publishes a prevention curriculum for grades four through six as well as public prevention and awareness information packets, videos, guides, and other materials.

National Association to Advance Fat Acceptance (NAAFA)
PO Box 22510, Oakland, CA 94609
Web site:www.naafa.org

NAAFA works through public education and activism to end weight-based discrimination and to improve the quality of life for overweight people. The association provides information about the disadvantages of weight-loss treatments and publishes the bimonthly *NAAFA Newsletter*.

Society for Adolescent Medicine (SAM)
1916 NW Copper Oaks Circle, Blue Springs, MO 64015

(816) 224-8010

Web site: www.adolescenthealth.org

SAM is a multidisciplinary organization of professionals committed to improving the physical and psychosocial health and well-being of all adolescents. It helps plan and coordinate national and international professional education programs on adolescent health. Its publications include the monthly *Journal of Adolescent Health* and the quarterly *SAM Newsletter*.

Web Sites

Teen Advice.Net (www.teenadvice.studentcenter.org). Teen Advice.Net offers teens expert and peer advice about health, body image, relationships, sexuality, gender issues, and other teen concerns.

TeensHealth (www.kidshealth.org/teen/nutrition/weight/dieting. html). TeensHealth was created for teens looking for honest, accurate information and advice about health, relationships, and growing up. TeensHealth's mission is to tell it to you straight.

Whole Family (www.wholefamily.com). Whole Family is designed for both parents and teens. The site's advice columnist, Liz, answers questions about body image, dieting, fitness, teen sex, drugs, drinking, and pregnancy, while online articles discuss other issues such as divorce, relationships, and health.

BIBLIOGRAPHY

Books

Robert, C. Atkins, *Dr. Atkins New Diet Revolution*. New York: Evans, 2002.

Kelly Brownell and Katherine Battle Horgen, *Food Fight: The Inside Story of the Food Industry, America's Obesity Crisis, and What We Can Do About It*. Chicago: Contemporary Books, 2004.

Deborah DeEugenio and Debra Henn, *Diet Pills: Drugs, the Straight Facts*. New York: Chelsea House, 2005.

Gina Kolata, *Rethinking Thin: The New Science of Weight Loss—and the Myths and Realities of Dieting*. New York: Farrar Straus & Giroux, 2007.

Don Kulick and Anne Meneley, *Fat: The Anthropology of an Obsession*. New York: Jeremy P. Tarcher/Penguin, 2005.

Phil McGraw, *The Ultimate Weight Solution: The 7 Keys to Weight Loss Freedom*. New York: Pocket Books, 2003.

Karen Miller-Kovach, *Weight Watchers: She Loses, He Loses: The Truth About Men, Women, and Weight Loss*. Indianapolis: Wiley, 2007.

Brandt Passalacqua,*Peaceful Weight Loss Through Yoga*. Lulu.com, 2005.

Michael Pollan, *The Omnivore's Dilemma*. New York: Penguin, 2006.

Joseph A. Resnick, *The Dark Side of Surviving Gastric Bypass Surgery: (What Doctors Don't Disclose)*. Frederick, MD: Publish America, 2007.

Kevin Trudeau, *The Weight Loss Cure They Don't Want You to Know About*. Elk Grove Village, IL: Alliance, 2007.

Periodicals

Associated Press, "Study: Low-Fat Tops Low-Carb for Keeping Pounds Off," *USA Today*, November 16, 2004.

Dan Brook, "Meat Is a Global Warming Issue," *E Magazine*, August 24, 2006.

Meghan Butryn and Thomas Wadden, "Treatment of Overweight Children and Adolescents: Does Dieting Increase Risk of Eating Disorders?" *International Journal of Eating Disorders*, May 2005.

Sophie Goodchild, "Dying to Be Thin," *Independent UK*, November 22, 2006.

Kathleen Goodwin, "Atkins Diet: A Comprehensive Analysis," *Diet Channel*, October 24, 2006.

Rachel Jones, "When Dieting Doesn't Work," *Essence*, August 2004.

Wayne C. Miller, "Exercise and Weight: Fit or Fat or Fit and Fat?" *Health at Every Size*, Summer 2005.

Marion Nestle, "Good Food," *AARP Magazine*, March–April 2007.

Catherine Orenstein, "The Dialectic of Fat," *Ms. Magazine*, Summer 2005.

Michael Pollan, "Unhappy Meals," *New York Times*, January 28, 2007.

Michele Simon, "Uncle Sam's Lame Diet Tips," *Alternet*, February 1, 2005.

Beth Schwartzapfel, "America's Growing Waistline," *WireTap*, January 19, 2006.

Marco Visscher, "You Do What You Eat," *Ode*, September 8, 2005.

Krista Walton, "American's Eating Disorder," *LA City Beat*, May 30, 2006.

Internet Sources

Carla K. Johnson, "Reading Diet Articles Could Be Unhealthy," Associated Press, January 2, 2007. www.boston.com/yourlife/health/fitness/articles/2007/01/02/reading_diet_articles_could_be_unhealthy.

Lesley Stahl, "African Plant May Help Fight Fat," CBS News, November 21, 2004. www.cbsnews.com/stories/2004/11/18/60minutes/main656458.shtml.

INDEX

PICTURE CREDITS

All photos © AP Images